PRISONERS ON T..... ....

Harold Churchill in India, 1941

Prisoners on the Kwai

Memoirs of Dr Harold Churchill

With extracts from the memories of
other ex-prisoners of war in the Far East

collected by Dr Sue Palmer

Lest We Forget Singapore

Larks Press

Published by the Larks Press
Ordnance Farmhouse
Guist Bottom, Dereham NR20 5PF
01328 829207

www.booksatlarkspress.co.uk
August 2005

Printed by the Lanceni Press
Garrood Drive, Fakenham

British Library Cataloguing-in-Publication Data
A catalogue record for this book is available
from the British Library.

ACKNOWLEDGEMENTS

This book would not have appeared without the tireless efforts of Dr Susan Palmer, who first wanted to get Harold Churchill's memoir into print, then, with the late Fred Hoskins, planned the FEPOW memorial in Dereham Market Place, and finally sought out and wrote down the memories of many ex-prisoners of war from the Dereham area of Norfolk.

The Publisher is grateful to Mr Robin Churchill for permission to print his father's memoir, for writing the Foreword and Introduction and for providing the photograph facing the title page.
Thanks are also due to the Dereham branch of FEPOW for permission to use pictures from their album of photographs.

ISBN 1 904006 27 2

Contents

Part One

Part Two

Maps and Illustrations

Maps drawn by David Yaxley
Drawings on pp. 103, 104 &116 are by Fred Hoskins

Part One: Foreword

Parts of this book had a long and chequered genesis. The main part consists of a memoir of his days as a Japanese prisoner of war in south-east Asia during World War 2 written by my father, Harold Churchill, in the years following his release from captivity.

My father's memoir is based on a diary, written on rice paper (now, I believe, in the Imperial War Museum), that he secretly kept during his captivity, even though the keeping of diaries was strictly prohibited by the Japanese. I believe that my father originally wrote his memoir as a form of therapy, to exorcise the ghosts of his war years, rather than with a view to publication. This is suggested by the closing lines of the first chapter and by the fact that my father constantly reworked his memoir. At least four different versions exist written in the first person, and there are also a number of versions written in semi-fictionalised, third-person format. Whether the version of the memoir presented here is the one that my father would have chosen to have had published, were he still alive today, it is impossible to know.

My father was a GP in a practice covering about ten scattered villages in south Norfolk. In the first few years following his return from the War, my father worked single-handed: only in the early 1950s did he acquire a partner. In those days the working life of a rural GP was very demanding. Home visits were the norm for my father; he did his own dispensing and, until he acquired a partner, he was on call 24 hours a day, seven days a week. There was thus very little time for writing. Most of the various version of the memoir were written early on Sunday mornings, usually before breakfast (throughout his life my father was an early riser) and always before going to church.

As well as the memoir, my father wrote a fragment of autobiography, covering the first decade of his life from 1906 to 1916. This has been included in this book partly because it sheds some light on the personality of my father and partly because it may have some general interest as my father's early years were rather unusual. Since the memoir begins a little abruptly and also refers without explanation to various people and places that will not be familiar to the general reader, I have written a short introduction that I hope will fill in a few gaps.

Although my father did not, I believe, originally set out to write his memoir for publication, he did make two or three unsuccessful attempts during his lifetime to get it published. Subsequently one of his friends, Dr Susan Palmer, who had read the memoir, directed some of her formidable energy into finding a publisher. My sisters and I are very grateful to her for her initiative and to Mrs Susan Yaxley of Larks Press for agreeing to publish it. Once it was likely that my father's memoir would be published, Susan Palmer interviewed a number of other Norfolk former Japanese PoWs about their wartime experiences, and these interviews make up the final part of this book.

Robin Churchill
Cardiff
January 2005

Harold Churchill Remembered
by Sue Palmer

As I think of Harold Churchill, what stands out is his old-fashioned courtesy. He never failed to stand up as I came into a room or as I left it. He always held the door open for a woman to pass through first.

Once, when he was doing morning surgery, it began to rain heavily and he hadn't brought his mac. I overheard him telephoning his wife. 'Helga, I believe you said you were coming into town this morning. Would it be too much trouble to ask you to bring my mackintosh, as it is beginning to rain?'

When we were seated round the dining table I noticed that Harold's plate was always clean at the end of the meal. He never left anything, other than a bone, on his plate. During a coffee break he would take time to savour his drink, and always sat with his hands curled round the mug to warm them.

He seldom spoke about his time as a prisoner, but I remember one story. A very sick man needed a blood transfusion; Harold found a donor by calling for volunteers, then mixing drops of blood from each, with that of the patient. If no obvious clotting occurred they went ahead. The donor and recipient were put next to each other on a bamboo platform and linked by the 'transfusion apparatus'. This consisted of two big thorns from a forest tree which had been hollowed out somehow by one of the clever prisoners in the camp, linked by a piece of tubing which had fixed a lorry windscreen in place.

He showed me his 'medical bag' once. It was a little metal box with a lid, about three inches by one and a half inches and perhaps an inch high in which was a tiny syringe and one morphine tablet. Medicine is a difficult skill at the best of times but this was ridiculous.

Malaria was rife, but there were quite inadequate supplies of quinine or atebrin to treat it, though the Japanese themselves had plenty. Dressings were so scarce that they had to be washed over and over again for re-use.

Harold was always trying to protect his sick men from being sent out on work parties, but not by any means always successfully.

Introduction

by Robin Churchill

As his fragment of biography recalls, Harold Churchill was born in 1906 in China, where his father was working as a medical missionary. This was at a time when China was still ruled by emperors, although the imperial dynasty was to end five years later. In 1910 Harold returned with his parents and two younger sisters to England. In 1912 the parents returned to China, leaving Harold and his sister Margaret (the aged four) behind. Both children were sent to boarding school, spending the school holidays with grandparents. It was another four years before the children saw their parents again.

From his early years Harold showed a keen interest in natural history, an interest that was to remain with him for the rest of his life. It was, as his memoir suggests, one of the major factors sustaining him throughout his captivity. One of the few books that he had with him during his prisoner-of-war years was a copy of Gilbert White's *The Natural History of Selborne*. He appears to have acquired it after he was captured, as the flyleaf is dated (in his handwriting) 'Singapore, May 1942'. His copy was a Penguin paper-back edition, published in 1941. This copy soon acquired a canvas binding, as the rear flyleaf records (again in Harold's handwriting) 'This book was bound by Pte A. Roberts, 2/Cambs. Regt, prisoner of war, at Changi on 12th August, 1942.' There is no mention of Private Roberts in Harold's memoir, so who he was remains a mystery – just one of hundreds of men that Harold came briefly into contact with during his three and a half years in captivity. The final 15 pages or so of this Penguin edition of *The Natural History*, which were originally blank, are covered in my father's small, neat handwriting. There are several verbatim extracts from E.J.H. Corwer's *Wayside Trees of Malaysia* (1940) and an extract from William McDougall's *An Outline of Psychology*. Whether these extracts were copied when Harold was a prisoner of war (and if so, from whom he borrowed the original books) or whether they were copied subsequently is impossible to know. There is also a brief chronology of his movements between different PoW camps.

When he left school in 1924, Harold was unsure what to do next. His academic interests lay in history and literature, but he was

3

persuaded by his father to follow in the latter's footsteps and become a doctor. Harold did his medical training at St Bartholomew's Hospital in London, and duly qualified in about 1931. After several years of hospital work and serving as a locum GP (including a period in Clare, Suffolk), he bought a medical practice based in the small Norfolk village of Pulham Market. Harold already knew Norfolk from his teen years, when his parents and their six children (who were then living in north London) had taken family holidays on the North Norfolk coast, Harold often cycling from London to get there. His spell as a locum in Clare further fostered his love of East Anglia.

In 1935 Harold met a 22-year old Norwegian girl called Helga Thommessen (the 'Helga' referred to several times in the memoir), who was living for a brief period in London at that time. Harold fell in love with her almost immediately, but his feelings were not reciprocated. At that time Helga was engaged to her childhood sweetheart, son of a Norwegian ship owner. Not put off, Harold met Helga a few more times before the outbreak of the war (including visiting her in Norway), but thereafter visits became impossible and correspondence difficult. Nevertheless Harold's feelings for Helga never wavered, and it was these, together with his love of nature and his deep religious faith, that kept him going mentally during the long years of captivity.

When the Second World War began in September 1939, Harold almost immediately joined the Home Guard in South Norfolk, but there was little for them to do beyond putting out the occasional fire. After Dunkirk, Harold wanted to do more to aid the war effort and therefore went to work in a military hospital in Edinburgh in July 1940, and then moved to Stranraer where he was also a medical officer. He did not feel that his work involved him sufficiently in the war effort, and so he volunteered for active service. He was sent to India in early 1941 (the convoy he was travelling in being attacked by German planes on the way). In India he was attached as a medical officer to the Indian Army. He spent nearly a year in India before being sent with the Punjabi Brigade to Singapore at the beginning of 1942. On the fall of Singapore on 15 February 1942 he was captured by the Japanese. He spent nearly a year in Singapore (mainly in Changi) before being taken to Thailand in November 1942 to work on the notorious Thai-Burma railway. From November 1942 to mid 1945 he worked as a doctor attending the large number of sick PoWs in various camps in Thailand, both at forest camps where the railway was being built and at the base camps at and close to a place called Kanburi (now known as Kanchanaburi). In the final months of the war he was sent to a place called Ubol (which may be the present-day Ubon) in eastern Thailand. At the end of September 1945 Harold and his fellow-prisoners were finally released and repatriated to Rangoon. He eventually arrived back in the United Kingdom on 9 November 1945.

As soon as he had returned to the United Kingdom, Harold was anxious to see Helga again, but was delayed by British and Norwegian bureaucracy, and so was not able to travel to Norway until early February 1946. Just over a fortnight later Harold and Helga were married at Tanum church, some 15 miles south of Oslo. They returned to Pulham Market, where Harold resumed the job of GP that he had left nearly six years earlier. They remained in Pulham until 1969, when they moved to Dereham. Harold died there in 1991, and Helga in 1995.

Any reader of Harold Churchill's memoir will be struck by its reticence. He does, of course, mention the deprivations and suffering that he and his fellow PoWs endured, but he does not dwell on them. He was also very reticent in talking about his wartime experiences for the rest of his life. Curiously, some of the things that he did talk about are not mentioned in the memoir. Thus he told us that to add some protein to the frequently rotting rice and vegetables that they were given by the Japanese, he and his fellow PoWs caught and ate ants. Occasionally, they were really lucky and managed to catch a snake. He reminded us of this sometimes with rather black humour. If, as happened from time to time, we children found an insect or a slug in the salad or the cabbage and complained, Harold would remark 'All good protein', occasionally referring to his consumption of insects as a PoW. He also occasionally spoke of the ingenuity of his fellow PoWs, for example of the man who had made a working clock entirely from bamboo. He also told us of fellow PoWs, who had been lecturers and teachers before the war, giving impromptu lectures in the evenings. Curiously, none of this is mentioned in the memoir.

His reluctance publicly to refer to his wartime experiences was manifested in other ways. He refused to join any Far Eastern PoW organisation. Although he went to church on Remembrance Sunday, he did so because he went to church every Sunday. At the Remembrance services he did not join the other PoWs, who sat together as a group, nor, unlike them, did he wear his medals. He did, however, keep in touch with some of his former fellow PoWs, and a few, including his old Indian colonel, came to visit him in Norfolk. Again curiously, none of these men, except the Indian colonel, is mentioned in his memoir, although it may be that he changed their names.

The Thai-Burma Railway near Hindati

1. From Norfolk to Bombay

In 1939, when the war began, I was living in the village of Pulham Market, in South Norfolk. On a Sunday morning, towards the end of harvest, the sun shone warmly, and in the fields on either side of the lane the corn was cut and ready for carting. At a railway level-crossing I met a farmer whom I knew; he was leaning heavily against the white-painted gate.

'Did you hear the news?' he asked as I came up. His big, good-humoured face was creased slightly by anxiety.

'Has the war started?' I asked in return.

'Yes,' he said, 'the Prime Minister spoke at eleven.'

He referred to Mr Chamberlain's broadcast. We stood talking for a few minutes in the sunshine, but in a sense a long journey had begun, for we had turned our backs already on the certainties of habit and custom.

In the evenings we saw the British bombers flying eastwards towards Germany. Later at night, if we woke, we heard the drone of their engines returning; the sound reached us from the distance behind the house, crossed over the orchard and paddock, and then died away. The sunny autumn was followed by a hard winter. The village continued in its usual occupations in the imagined security of the Maginot Line. In May 1940, when France fell, we prepared for invasion by blocking the roads and at nights we watched the seaward sky from a hill-top. My turn of watching was from eleven till one; my companions were men of the village, sometimes a younger man, sometimes a veteran of the 1914 war. When we separated I walked home through the churchyard under the shadow of the tower. But soon - I was the village doctor and unmarried - I left familiar scenes. I went to the Depot of the R.A.M.C. at Leeds, and from there I was sent to Edinburgh to learn my duties at the military hospital in the castle.

The Scottish capital was enjoying fine weather. Seen from the Castle Hill, the small figures of the crowds in Princes Street seemed to have a gaiety and a liveliness, derived perhaps from the sunshine. At the castle the colonel gave us a lecture on the philosophy of war, speaking to us in a stone-flagged room where pikes and halberds rested against the walls. In the distant past, he said, simple peoples had lived peacefully in isolated communities; but as their cultures improved they developed ideals, and when the ideals and the self-interest of neighbouring communities were in conflict, war resulted. He was a distinguished man and had been a professor at the university.

From here I was sent for a few days to a coastal defence battery on the island of Inchcolm, in the Firth of Forth. The air was moist with a drizzle of rain as I stepped from the boat onto the jetty. Little waves splashed on the iron boom. A sentry looked at my pass, and with a gesture muffled by his cape he pointed to the line of huts where the C.O. lived. I tapped at a door and was met by a young officer who introduced himself as the mess-secretary. He showed me a camp-bed in the hut where I was to sleep and left me looking at a row of torn paperbacks suspended on a little shelf above it.

The following night an air-raid alarm roused us. I pulled on my trousers and boots. Coming down the steps into the darkness, I could distinguish the shapes of soldiers hurrying along the narrow paths to the guns. In the silence the sound of the tide was discernible, washing slowly against the rocks. I made my way to the centre of the island, where a small abbey survived the monks who had built it; its chapter-house was used as a first-aid post. An electric bulb hung on a wire from the fan-vaulting and lit the white faces and clumsy bodies of the stretcher-bearers. We waited, but nothing happened.

When the war was finished a friend told me of the fighting at Cape Anzio in Italy; in the intervals of the gunfire, he said, when there was a moment's suspension of the din, they heard the nightingales singing in a wood. But here there was no gunfire and there were no nightingales. I left the men to their sleepy conversation and walked out into the darkness. I felt a warm wind on my temples and smelt the herbs of the cloister-garden.

I was posted away from Edinburgh. The train travelled slowly across a moor. The slopes of the ground were covered with heather and bracken. Further on, trees, pastures and farm-buildings gave variety to the landscape. At the little stations, consisting of a single platform, the clumps of pink roses which grew against the yellow palings were lifted and tossed by the wind. The grey sky became darker. Finally the train reached the harbour of Stranraer, and drew up on the pier. The wind had increased to a gale, and the white crests of the waves moved rapidly towards the shore. I found the embarkation officer in a wooden hut. 'I'll tell you the way to town,' he said, 'but I can't come with you. I must see the troops onto the ship.' I found my way through the dark cobbled streets to a small hotel.

The next morning I reported for duty at Movement Control Head-quarters. The embarkation of troops was done mainly at nights, when the long railway trains bringing soldiers from London and the Midlands ran directly onto the pier.

The embarkation staff waited in a small stuffy office, warmed by a coal-fire, the cast-iron fender of which bore the motto 'No place like home'. At a desk in a corner an elderly corporal wrote laborious, long letters to his wife with a pen that scratched the lines. The embarkation officer read the newspaper, scanning a single sheet at a time and keeping the remainder folded in the pocket of his greatcoat. A bell buzzed sharply; at the signal the corporal pushed the cork into his ink-bottle and the embarkation officer buttoned up the neck of his greatcoat. The two men went out into the darkness, sniffing the salt air of the bay. They listened for the faint sounds of a ship's engines.

The troops awaiting embarkation stood in six or eight ranks close to the edge of the pier. They stood in silence, for the darkness made them drowsy. They were clad in heavy greatcoats and carried rifles, kit-bags and packs. One night I remember in particular. The wind blew chilly across the harbour. The hum of a ship's engines and the thrashing of its screws were heard, and the little blue navigation-lights could be seen moving slowly towards the pier. 'Here she comes,' said a soldier standing directly above the water. He turned, with a careless movement of his feet, and was gone, dropping from sight into the waves that washed the stakes and girders beneath. The man who had stood next to him flung his rifle and pack to his neighbour. 'Hold these,' he said briefly and shook himself free of his greatcoat. Then he jumped, disappearing into the darkness.

The shaded blue lights of the ship drew close to the pier; the sound of its engines ceased. A voice cried from the waves beneath, 'Throw a rope!' The black hulk of the ship was very close now, blocking the view. The powerful voice cried again from below, 'Throw a rope!' The plates of the ship's side touched the edge of the pier very gently and the ship came to rest. A rope had been thrown, and the two men were safe. The embarkation of troops could now begin.

After five months the work on the pier and at the transit-camp became very monotonous, and I asked the C.O.'s permission to volunteer for overseas service. The C.O. was a quiet-mannered man, wearing the ribbon of the D.S.O., which he had won as a subaltern on the Somme in 1916. He sat at his desk, looking with blue, tolerant eyes across the bay, where two transport-ships lay anchored. After listening to my request he began to speak of the management and breeding of pigs. 'You live in the country, don't you?' he asked. I repeated my request, and he allowed it.

My leave was spent with my parents at Broxbourne, in Hertfordshire. The train passed over the bridge into the station with a hollow rumble; the riverside willows were leafless. At home the warm curtains were drawn. My father sat reading *The Spectator* in an armchair by the fire, my mother was writing letters. At this time air-raids were frequent.

'Here they come,' said my mother quietly, with just a touch of distaste in her voice, when the thump-thump of anti-aircraft guns began to be heard. I happened to go early into London the morning after an incendiary raid. The shops and warehouses of St Paul's Churchyard and Paternoster Row had been gutted by fire; their broken walls stood up roofless and charred. The firemen, who had worked all night, were leaving the scene; their feet stumbled on the wet pavements as they dragged and coiled the heavy lengths of their hose-pipes. Their faces were white with exhaustion under the black marks of smoke and soot. But in a tea-shop the girl standing behind the counter was cheerful. 'I'm off on Monday,' she called over her shoulder to someone out of sight. 'I'm working on Sunday, but I'm off duty all day on Monday.' She wore a black dress with white lace at the wrists and neck.

Returning from leave, I crossed London to catch an early evening train to the North. The taxi-driver who drove me sat humped behind his wheel, with a muffler flung loosely round his neck. The sky over London was dark, and the streets, in which neither windows nor streetlamps showed any glimmer of light, were almost empty of people. An air-raid began; and the broken walls of houses, bombed in previous raids, showed naked against the flashes of gunfire. Beneath the roof of the station the porters were loading luggage into a train by the light of small blue points. A subaltern, leaning from the window of a railway carriage, was joking with two girls who looked up at him from the platform. A fire began to burn in the direction of the docks, lighting up a fragment of the sky. The taxi-driver, a man with a shaggy moustache, said, 'We must all die once, but it is not certain that we shall die of old age.' He moved away into the dusk.

※

When at last the convoy was ready, it sailed from Liverpool in the late afternoon. The next morning the sun rose astern, above the Mull of Kintyre, mounting through flakes of pink cloud into a blue sky. As I stood on the deck I looked across the water to cold hill-tops, whitened by snow. Sometimes an escort vessel, a destroyer or corvette, raced with a dash of foam between the merchant-ships.

The ships had set out in a long, curving line but now they moved in parallel columns, plunging steadily through the waves. Sometimes a ripple of coloured flags broke out at a masthead to signal an order. The passengers, who were all men and mainly civilians, came up from below and paced the seamed planks in twos and threes. For some moments a floating mine bobbed like a black and glistening berry between the ships; and the men, having nothing to do, ran to the ship's side to see it pass.

The weather changed, and trickles of rain streaked the glass of the portholes. Under cover of the clouds a Fokker-Wolff Kondor aircraft attacked the convoy. At the sound of gunfire all the men in the saloon jumped up and ran outside. We saw the Kondor wheeling above the masts of a vessel whose deck seemed to bulge and break into smoke. The plane flew over the convoy, turned and attacked again, its second bomb throwing up a spout of water near one of the destroyers. The guns rattled angrily but the Kondor swerved aside and climbed out of sight.

I had stood watching the machine-gunner on our poop, who at each approach of the Kondor had added his own rat-tat-tat to the din. At the finish the gunner took his stand in the open, bareheaded, cursing and shaking his fist at the clouds. His gun, which had jammed, was the ship's only weapon. A little group of seamen had come together close by me, and I heard one of them, a dusky Lascar, ask 'Was it a German plane?' 'Yes,' replied another, an Englishman, 'and you can bet that he will soon come back with some of his friends.' The seamen stood swollen and misshapen in their blue kapok life jackets, while the wind fluttered the thin trousers at their ankles.

The English sailor was right. An hour before dusk, the attack was resumed by four Kondors, which roared, machine-gunning and bombing, above the ships. The bullets tore through the ropes that held a lifeboat and splintered the deck at my feet. The vessel lurched and rolled sharply as a bomb burst alongside, and I staggered. Close by, I saw an oil-tanker sinking stern-first. Beyond it another was burning, and as the steel plates crumpled and fell apart the sea-water surged in. Further back, a third vessel emitted a murky smoke, shot through with flames. In all, twelve ships went down.

As the ships sank, humanity seemed to be extinguished. No crews had been seen to run onto the decks to lower the boats or to throw themselves into the sea. It was left to the imagination to hear the hissing of steam in the engine-rooms, to notice the sudden silence of the engines and to be appalled by the cries of the men trapped below. One of the escorting destroyers had let down a cutter to look for survivors; its oars rose and fell on the waves - but, so far as I could see, no survivors were found.

Shortly before dusk the attack ceased when the attacking Kondors drew off. The men in the *Elysia* went below decks to drink cocoa from steaming mugs. As they sat at the long tables beneath the hanging lamps (some wearing blue jerseys, some tweed jackets, only a few in khaki) they talked gently and turned warm, friendly faces to each other. During the night the convoy dispersed, so that when I came on deck in the morning I saw nothing but the tossing grey sea and the Atlantic waves which broke thudding and swirling over the fo'c'sle.

A week later the mountains of Sierra Leone were sighted, their tops clothed with mist and their lower slopes patterned green and red by the vegetation and the soil. The ship glided into the broad anchorage of Freetown, and its engines stopped.

The same evening the moon rose full and round, throwing black shadows among the silvered roofs and open squares of the town. The air was warm, inviting the passengers onto the deck. A young engineer throbbed a tune on a ukulele. The ship's derricks stood angularly beside the mast; a rope creaked as a Lascar hauled it taut. I stood by the rail in the shadow of a lifeboat, in

11

conversation with an officer of a parachute regiment. 'You can do what you please with your life,' he remarked, 'but death is the end.' I said nothing; I was unwilling to agree but I was unprepared to give any good reason. We were silent for a moment and then we resumed our talk on a different topic.

2. India

The voyage ended at Bombay. As the ship approached the harbour the local fishing-fleet came out in a haze of spray, pitching through the waves under top-heavy sails. I stood watching them with an Indian law-student returning from London. 'You have been friendly during the voyage,' said the Indian, 'but when we go ashore you will not want to speak to me. In India I belong to the subject race.' Two days later, by chance, I saw him in one of the narrow streets of Bombay. I crossed the road, with hand outstretched, but the Indian turned proudly away, without speaking.

I travelled inland by the Frontier Mail. Although it was night the air of the compartment was warm, and a hot dust was blown in through the window. At daybreak I looked from the train and saw monkeys scrambling over a rocky slope. The landscape that moved past me belonged to the early days of the world's history, recalling the Old Testament patriarchs. A bullock-cart, which carried its driver humped on the shafts, went swaying along a field-track; some women came with empty water-pots to a well. At a halt a young woman in a faded red sari held a child by the hand; the child's thin legs were blotched and scabby. 'Poverty is the curse of India,' said the other occupant of the carriage, an Indian.

My destination was Mhow, a small garrison-town in Central India. The great stone barracks, built in 1840 for the East India Company, had stood half-empty since the start of the war in North Africa, when the British regiment usually stationed in Mhow had been sent to Libya. I lived at the English Club, sleeping out-of-doors at nights beneath a gul-mohur tree, whose flame-like petals I saw between myself and the sky when I awoke. During the day I worked as a junior medical officer in the military hospital, where the Indian medical orderlies loitered until they were called for, in the shade of a verandah. The hot sunshine beat down on the red dust of the courtyard and on the deep green leaves of a peepul-tree. One sultry midday, while I was at the hospital, the driver of a staff-car drew up with a jerk at the entrance and ran in with a message. Could a medical officer come at once? A mishap had occurred among a party of military cadets who had gone bathing. I sprang into the car and was driven away from the town along a rough country road. After four or five miles the car stopped at a lakeside, where a group of young

Indians stood silently. Close to them a broad-shouldered body lay face downwards in the shallow water. I splashed to it in my boots, caught the body beneath the armpits and pulled it onto the firmer ground. But I had come too late, the cadet had drowned among the reeds. As I straightened myself up, my eyes looked across the wide water of the lake, which sparkled at innumerable points as its surface was rippled by a light wind. At a distance a range of hills was surmounted by a long white cloud, spread motionless in the blue sky. Within a hundred yards of me, on the surface of the lake, a flock of waterfowl was feeding quietly.

In the evenings I sat on the lawn at the Club, one of the little circle of women and men who talked less of the war than of the small day-to-day events of the place. On occasions the band of a neighbouring rajah came and, standing on the grass beneath the illuminations, played military marches. More often the evenings were quiet, and at the far end of the lawn the weak lights of fireflies danced and flickered in front of a shrubbery whose darkness was impenetrable.

Only rarely, when my work was finished, I walked through the single narrow street of the native town. The surface of the road was sandy and soft underfoot, so that the people passing to and fro on bare feet walked silently. The darkness of night surrounded their little houses; only the shop-fronts, open to the road, were illumined by yellow points of light. The counters displayed food, both cooked and uncooked, cotton fabrics and cheap aluminium ware from Japan. Rarely a pony-cart trotted by, with a jingle of bells and a smell of sweat from the pony. The men flitting in white shirts between the shadows passed without speaking; the women, too, whose saris had become sombre-coloured, moved soundlessly. Men and women alike looked at me with sad, suspicious eyes, or turned their glances away. Is this, I asked myself, what it is to belong to the ruling race?

At the end of three months I left Mhow with orders to go to Poona. For some moments as the train moved slowly I looked down from the high bridge over the Narbadda river and saw the snake-like trickle of water in its gorge between the trees. At a midnight halt I watched an Indian soldier take leave of his family. The soldier's wife knelt at his feet on the station platform, wailing softly; his children clung silently to his knees. A hanging oil-lamp dulled the mauves and reds of the women's saris and the dusky faces of the men behind them. The soldier, wearing a greenish-khaki uniform, held himself stiffly, his face glistening beneath the oil-lamp, as he stared with a fixed look into the distance. A garland of white flowers hung in a loop from his shoulders. The leave-taking was prolonged by some need to refuel the engine, or to supply water; then, as an official shouted in the darkness, the man turned and climbed deliberately, because of the weight of his kit, into the carriage.

13

At Poona I joined an Indian Army Field Ambulance in training. It was a unit of three hundred and fifty officers and men. The C.O., Col. Dutta, was a Bengali from Calcutta, who had made a reputation as a civil surgeon in the Punjab. He was a small, eager man with brown eyes and a pleasant smile. I watched him through a whole morning during the court-martial of an ambulance-sepoy who had absconded. He had sold his uniform, he said, and gone to live with a woman in the native city until she could no longer afford to keep him. The colonel listened attentively and sent him back to his village without punishment. 'I am not going to take anyone overseas with me,' he said, 'who does not come willingly.' The second-in-command, an Englishman with a regular army commission, protested. 'Sir,' he said, 'the man has disgraced the King's uniform and he ought to be horse-whipped.' He was critical also of the junior Indian officers, Pillai, Unny and Chinchvad. Although they had volunteered, they had no real liking for the military life. As Unny said, smiling, 'This life is very strange. At home I get up in the morning and when I have bathed, I go to the temple. The temple is in our garden.' The rank and file of the unit were recruits from all the provinces of India, speaking many different languages (our common tongue was Urdu); some were Hindus, some were Musselmans. They lived in a friendly way together, although by village tradition the two creeds should have been separate. They ate different food and had their separate cook-houses.

We spent six months in Poona. The brick-built and mud-floored barracks of the Field Ambulance stood close to the Poona racecourse, separated by a sandy road and some acacia trees. Our time was occupied in training our recruits, collecting equipment and learning to use everything. We went for prolonged exercises in the surrounding countryside. My havildar, marching beside me, explained the methods of cultivating the land. His name was Hiralal; a farmer's son, he was friendly and intelligent. The dusty roads, the bullocks drawing the water from the wells, the narrow fields, became familiar sights. Once we crossed a river at dusk and came to an ancient walled village of the Marathis; the citadel was deserted, its enclosure overgrown with grass and thorny acacias. Returned to Poona, my relaxation when work was finished was to walk in the Botanical Gardens, pacing the gravelled paths between the flowerbeds and the shady cassia and casuarina trees. Once or twice I went to the river-bank and looked across the troubled brown water to the grey walls of Poona jail, where the Indian leader, Mahatma Gandhi, was a prisoner.

At the end of November we left Poona, marching out in the dust raised by the three Punjabi battalions that went ahead of us. A curving road led us up the ascent of Deva Ghat and away from the country which was familiar to us. The hills were bare; they had been scorched by the sunlight of many centuries. We slept on the open ground, beneath a clear sky. At first I looked up at the

14

constellation of Orion; when I woke later Cassiopeia was overhead, but the whole sky was glistening. In the morning half-light a hawk flew above me, its under-parts bronzed by the sun, which was still below the horizon. By daylight I saw that I had slept near a native shrine. It was no more than a heap of grey stones, roughly shaped and unevenly put together, on which a handful of flowers had been placed and now lay fading. The young Indian officer named Unny approached. 'Don't despise the flowers,' he said, 'they are placed there by the peasants who believe with Mahatma Gandhi that the world is God's playground and reflects his glory. Those are Mahatma Gandhi's own words.'

The brigade and divisional exercises began. We travelled in line, jolting along the bullock-tracks, while the dust arose like smoke from the wheels of the vehicles. It was a parched countryside, with cultivation only in the region of the canals and the wells. There were frequent stoppages, when we heard the sad sound of the wind rustling in the crops, which had withered from drought. We came to a grey-walled village; about half of the buildings were roofless, and the stones lay in tumbled heaps, over which the goats scrambled. At the centre of the village a group of men squatted by the well to watch the convoy of lorries go by. Women leant against the doorposts with babies in their arms, and a few older children were playing. At dusk we halted; the lorries were dispersed, their drivers taking them in all directions across the cornfields. The cooks lighted their fires.

The officers sat together under a big-branched mango-tree, the lamp on the table showing an irregular group of faces. Beyond the circle of its light the darkness was velvety. After supper I picked up my hurricane lamp, which swung in my hand as I walked, and went round the cornfield to see my company. The cooks' fire was dying; the men lay around it in the corn, wrapped in their blankets and already asleep. We moved off in the morning. The farmer, a stout man dressed in a loose, white garment and a red turban, stood on a dyke to survey his fields. They were scored and criss-crossed by the lorry-tracks. 'First God sends the drought,' he remarked to a passing sepoy, 'and then he sends the soldiers!'

The midday halt was made by a well, in open country with a shallow, stony soil. Some steps inside the well led down to the water, which lay partly in shade, partly in sunshine. The men asked permission to bathe. Some went down the steps but many jumped from the top, dropping feet-first into the water and sending up spouts of glittering water-drops. The hollow of the well rang with their shouts and laughter.

3. To Singapore

The whole brigade and its accessories embarked and sailed together from Bombay. Our destination was Singapore, already threatened by the Japanese advance through Malaya. We followed an indirect route to the west and south of Sumatra, before turning north through the Sundra and Banka Straits. We saw the shores of Sumatra, low and barely rising out of the water on one side, the hills and forests of Java on the other. The numerous smaller islands seemed all alike; the trees grew down to the water, the fishermen's huts stood on stakes in the shallows. Our approach to Singapore was covered by squalls of rain. Japanese bombers, we were told, had flown over in the morning, but our ships docked safely; we came ashore at a quiet wharf in the Naval Harbour and marched out to the lorries which were waiting to take us away.

Singapore is a hilly island, covered with vegetation and having a red, clayey soil. The road from the Naval Harbour ran between plantations of rubber trees; Chinese settlements were strung along the length of it. We saw parties of stragglers and deserters from the campaign on the mainland. The lorries put us down near the village of Jurong, in the western half of the island. Some tents had been pitched for us in a plantation. It was raining again, but the cooks lighted fires and made tea, and so we settled ourselves for the night. In the morning the wet canvas of the tents soon dried in the sunlight. We unloaded our gear. At ten o'clock in the morning a formation of Japanese bombers appeared, flying at a considerable height. We listened to the thud and crash of their bombs on Tangah aerodrome, two miles away. The men were excited, lying on the ground beneath the trees, but finding themselves unhurt, they showed their relief by making small jokes among themselves. After this attack on Tangah aerodrome the R.A.F. were withdrawn from the island, leaving it without defence in the air except for a few anti-aircraft guns.

While the men lived in tents, the officers of the Field Ambulance shared a wooden barn on the edge of the plantation. Here we were in close and strained contact with one another. The second-in-command was brusque and demanding towards the younger Indian officers, who responded with a sulky resentment. 'I'm tired of these silly squabbles,' Col. Dutta said to me one night, as we paced up and down the road after supper, 'let's talk of something pleasanter.' We planned a trip to Kashmir, to take place after the war. He and his wife, whom I had known in Poona, had spent many holidays there. Our part of the road was in shadow; nearby, in the brilliant moonlight, two British soldiers were uncoiling the wire of a field telephone. As we talked, a big gun rolled up and unlimbered under the trees. After a short interval, it was followed by another. The evacuation of the mainland was now complete, and the causeway between Singapore and Johore was shortly afterwards blown up.

The next morning we woke to hear the firing of a heavy gun on the north side of the island. The Japanese advance troops had reached the Johore Strait.

The Punjabi brigade-sector was fourteen miles off the coast on the western extremity of the island; it was mainly swamp, and without any prepared defences. On our right, two Australian brigades faced the mainland across the narrow strait; and on the left a Malay regiment lined the Jurong creek. Tuas, a village in the Punjabi sector, was perhaps typical. Trees grew in the water, and the water penetrated the land through narrow channels of mud. A small landing stage had been used by the fishermen. The wooden houses standing close to it showed the signs of a hasty departure; inside the half-open doors, clothes, shoes and scraps of paper littered the floors. The population had all left. In the open street I saw an Australian captain interrogating four British soldiers who had come ashore at the jetty. Gaunt, unshaven and ragged, they had navigated a sampan precariously down the coast after being separated from their unit in the jungle-fighting in the north. The sepoys of the Punjabi battalions worked hard, wading into the water and pulling barbed wire across the creeks, where the meeting of sea and land was indeterminate. At night they patrolled their defences.

The Australians had already seen some hard fighting in Malaya. One morning as Col. Dutta and I walked over a piece of open ground, we came across two of their machine-gunners lying in the long grass beside their weapon. 'Are you getting ready to have another whack at the Japanese?' asked the colonel in his friendly way. 'We've seen enough of the Japs,' said one of them wearily. Perhaps he had been sickened of killing men.

At Jurong village the Field Ambulance was five miles from the coast, so the Colonel sent my company forward to establish a dressing-station nearer to the Punjabis. Here we lived in tents in a narrow rubber-plantation at the base of a hill, the top of which gave a view from one end of Singapore Island to the other; the harbour and ships in one direction, the blue sea and green coasts all round. Only the channel separating us from the mainland was hidden; but its position was marked by a column of smoke, which rose from the bombed and burning petrol-tanks of the Naval Base. My dressing-station was a small, whitewashed wooden shed; our vehicles stood under the thicker trees near-by. The evenings were peaceful. When we had washed ourselves and eaten our supper we sat and watched the nightjars flying over the path that led to the village of Lockyang.

On the night of 8 February, soon after dark, heavy gunfire began on the north side of the island. The ground on which we lay shook beneath us, and sleep was impossible. In any momentary lull the myriad voices of frogs asserted themselves, croaking in the water-channels of the Lockyang market gardens. The morning, like all these mornings, came fresh and bright. The

17

cannonade ceased, but Japanese planes were soon active. Three of them flew low enough to machine-gun us through the trees.

At about eleven o'clock Col. Dutta came to our dressing-post. 'Have you heard anything from Pasir Laba?' he asked.

'No,' I said.

'The Japanese made a landing there last night among the Australians. You must be ready to move at short notice.'

Soon afterwards, our position was bombed. We lay on the ground listening to the swish and thump of the missiles, which fell close to us. As we got to our feet a British soldier came up on a motorcycle, stripped to the waist, his face pale and streaked with dirt. 'We want some help. Our gun-position has been bombed. Can you come?' I took an ambulance-car and drove after him. About a mile away we came to the guns. The trees around them were uprooted and torn, as if lashed by a hurricane; the ground was pitted, and a grey dust had fallen on everything. A soldier lay on his face, just as he had flung himself when the attack came, but his cheek, turned upwards to the sun, was cold and ashy. A second gun-position, deeper in the plantation, had received the same treatment. Six men in all were dead, and five were wounded. I had with me a Marathi orderly, whose eyes, I noticed, were compassionate. We worked together until we had got the wounded men into the ambulance, and drove away. I left the ambulance at the road, after directing its driver to the rear, and returned to the dressing-station on foot.

The men were standing under the trees with their kit in bundles at their feet. An order had come from Col. Dutta to leave in half an hour's time. I had only one lorry to take all the equipment as well as the sixty men. It made several journeys, but half the company marched, and I marched with them. A bomb-crater in the road had blocked the vehicles; and shortly beyond it we were machine-gunned from the air, so we took to a path through the plantations. It began to rain. A platoon of Punjabi infantry were jumping out of their trucks to take up a new defensive position. We reached the Jurong brickworks and were told that Col. Dutta was at brigade-headquarters. The young Indian officer named Unny was in charge. The rest of the unit were sitting in the lorries, ready to move. We overtook an Indian labour-battalion, retiring on foot. Most of them still carried their shovels but they had broken ranks and were running. The rain streamed down their faces, upturned to us as we passed them. Our lorries pulled up on the lawns of a large European house, where we ran the vehicles under the trees and prepared for the night. The house was unlighted; and in the darkness we heard on the main road the whirring wheels of lorries and the shouts of their drivers as they called to each other.

At one point on the coast, on a small promontory jutting out from the

18

mangrove-swamps, a young subaltern of artillery had stayed by his gun. Behind him was the open sea; in front was the strait, which carried the Japanese landing-craft from the mainland. Alone with his weapon, he had aimed and fired and reloaded it for some hours as the little boats crossed. The Japanese, it seemed, were unwilling to turn aside from their main task in order to silence him. When his ammunition was finished, he dismantled his gun and stepped into the small rowing boat which he had kept by him. By now the coasts were almost hidden in the darkness. He rowed in silence, hearing only the dipping of his oars, until eventually, almost exhausted, he swung his boat into the Jurong creek and jumped ashore.

❋

The battle that followed the Japanese landing on Singapore was confused. On the second morning, soon after daybreak, the Japanese planes began to bomb and machine-gun the defenders. At midday the Japanese infantry renewed their attack. The Field Ambulance set up dressing-posts to which the wounded men were brought, some on stretchers, some walking. The noise from machine-guns and mortar bombs increased. My dressing-post was attacked from the air, perhaps because close behind it a British anti-aircraft gun was firing. Its shells flew overhead to burst harmlessly around the Japanese aircraft. At dusk the Field Ambulance moved back to a position nearer the city; and a hot, restless night was passed beneath the verandahs of another big European house.

The next morning I was sent forward again with three ambulance-cars to the brigade headquarters. The road was deserted and quiet, bathed in sunshine. At a turn of the road I found the brigadier and his staff leaning against a high bank of earth, shaded by trees, with a trickle of water slipping beneath their boots. A short distance ahead, but out of sight, rifles and machine-guns could be heard firing. A ditch on the other side of the road was filled with wounded Indians. I began, with the young Indian medical officer who had come with me, to dress their wounds. An Australian runner appeared beside me. 'We have a badly-wounded man on the hill-top,' he said, 'can you come?' I followed him onto a bare slope across which, from time to time, a bullet strayed, but halfway up we were met by a stretcher-party, carrying the wounded man. I knelt by the stretcher as they lowered it and gave the wounded man morphia. In the afternoon the brigade fell back a thousand yards and took up a line at the top of an open hillside. An Indian soldier dropped into the grass beside me. 'Sahib,' he said, 'when will the battle cease?' He was young, but his limbs were heavy with fatigue. At dusk patrols were sent forward and the remainder of the brigade prepared to sleep. During the night an ammunition-truck and a ration-lorry came up in the darkness, and were unloaded by the staff-captain and myself, in order to avoid waking the tired men.

The day that followed began quietly. I walked to a road where a water-lorry had been driven into a ditch and left there as a wreck. A young English officer, whom I knew slightly, approached from the opposite direction. 'Good morning,' he said pleasantly, 'may I join you?' We filled our water-bottles at the tap of the water-truck, and rinsed our hands and faces. 'At home,' said the other, 'on a fine morning like this we would hear three or four skylarks singing.' His home, I think he said, was a village in East Suffolk near the coast. 'Do you know that part of the country?' he asked, before continuing his way up the road. An hour later the forward company, to which he belonged, was ambushed, and almost all were killed.

Mortar bombs from either side now flew overhead with a curious whistling sound. Any movement on the hillside drew the fire of the Japanese planes that quartered the slope. At night the brigade was ordered to retire, and the troops moved off into the darkness. I stayed, because a stretcher party, sent out to find a wounded man, had not yet returned. I sat waiting in the driver's seat of an ambulance-car. The sky had become overcast, the wind cool. I listened and heard nothing. An hour passed, and I thought, 'They will never find me now in this darkness.' But I heard a sound behind me, some whispered words and a grunt as a stretcher was lowered to the ground; the wounded man groaned. I started my engine and drove slowly, without lights, along a sandy track. On coming to the road I overtook a battalion of British infantry filing quietly down the grass verges, their rifles slung over their shoulders.

When daylight came, I looked at the wounded man in the ambulance-car I had driven. There was a deep sadness in his eyes. He said nothing. Then I recognised him; he was the young sepoy who had dropped down in the grass beside me on the hillside, asking 'When will the battle cease?'

The new position taken up by the Punjabi brigade was known as the Buona Vista Road. For most of the day the Indian troops rested in a plantation, where they were joined by the survivors of two English regiments, the East Surreys and the Leicesters, who had fought up country. In the afternoon I left my company there and made my way back to Col. Dutta's headquarters. I drove along roads whose surfaces had been cut up by bombing, and saw the telephone wires on either side hanging loosely from the poles. I found the Field Ambulance headquarters in the stable of a house near the city. On being told that Col. Dutta was busy, I sat down to wait, staring up at the cobwebs in the fanlight above the door. An anti-aircraft gun nearby began to fire, and bombs fell further away in the city. Soon afterwards Col. Dutta came in, followed by Unny. 'Let's have something to eat,' he said; 'we have been at work since daybreak. Unny had never told us that he is a first-class anaesthetist, but we have discovered it for ourselves.'

We sat down at an old card-table with a green moth-eaten top on which an orderly placed coffee and sandwiches. Unny seemed quiet and thoughtful. 'Pillai is dead,' Col. Dutta told me, 'he was hit by a fragment of bomb yesterday.' I knew that Pillai had been a friend, at one time a fellow-student, of Unny. The colonel added, 'I do not think that most of us will come out of this alive. I am sorry for our men; they have no quarrel with the Japanese.' He was silent for a moment, then he added, 'We must not give up hope.'

I returned to the plantation where I had left the Punjabis. A few mortar bombs had fallen among them, causing some casualties. But the order had come to retire again, and the Indians began, one company after another, to move quietly out into the dusk. I decided to stay with the rearguard, made up of British troops, only keeping Hiralal, my ever-dependable havildar, and a few stretcher-bearers with me.

The rearguard waited among the trees until midnight; then, in the darkness, they rose to their feet, slung their rifles over their shoulders and stepped out of the plantation. They carried their bayonets naked on their rifles. I had slept a little and was still drowsy. As we crossed some swampy ground I stumbled and would have fallen from a plank-bridge but Hiralal, marching in front of me, swung round and caught my arm to steady me. I heard the sound of a boot striking a stone as we came to firmer ground. We climbed by a path through another plantation and filed along a railway-track, where the fire of a burning petrol-store lit up the marching men. Immense clouds of smoke, in which the red flames darted capriciously, rolled upwards into the sky from the burning tanks. The rearguard joined the brigade in the grounds of a large empty house, called Mount Echo, where they waited for daybreak. The house had been looted, and silk dresses, shoes and scarves, dragged from the cupboards, lay in disorder on the floors.

Here we were bombarded for the next two days, at first by low-flying aircraft and then by the Japanese big guns. I lay flat on a lawn as the shelling became fiercer. I heard the whistle of shells and saw spouts of earth flung up around me as the shells burst. I watched, close by me, a small bird creeping between the green leaves of a bush, whose flowers were scarlet. Then bird, bush and flowers disappeared in a flash of light. I shut my eyes against this sudden brilliance. When I opened them again I saw the blood running from my mouth onto my shirt. As I looked up I saw Hiralal's anxious face and heard his voice, full of concern, asking 'Sahib, are you hurt?'

An hour later the British commander in Singapore surrendered, judging perhaps that the civilian population could endure no more. Their crowded and flimsy houses had given them no protection from the Japanese bombs and shells. A day or two before the end I had myself seen some Chinese searching the wreckage of their homes. As they scrambled over the splintered planks, a woman stood upright in a doorway, holding across her arms the limp body of a child. The child's dress was the colour of a poppy flower. The woman's mouth was open as if to utter a cry of grief, but no sound came from her.

Conquest

These roads are dead
Strips of greyness between
The coconut palms.
The atap shed,
The white cupola,
Alike are shams.

Their walls are hollows
Where dust grows, breathless,
On spiders' webs.
The wells are shallow,
Their sides have fallen,
The water ebbs.

All troops have passed,
All tanks, trucks, lorries;
Their impulse spent.
Fringing the forest,
The dead await
The next event

4. Capitulation

After the capitulation of Singapore the British troops marched out of the city on Japanese orders, and only some of the wounded were allowed to remain. The Union Jack Club, to which I had been taken, was in use as a makeshift hospital. An Indian medical officer, a friend of Col. Dutta, was in charge; the nursing-orderlies and most of the patients were Indians. Food, dressings and drugs were all in short supply. When some lorries standing in front of the building had been bombed, the window-curtains and the mosquito nets above the beds had caught fire, and they still hung, charred and sooty. The yard was littered with the wreckage of burnt-out lorries. On the other side of the square some Eurasian children lived in the flats above a cinema. They were not allowed to go into the streets, but in the evenings they stood crowded together on the fire escape, jumping impatiently on their toes.

One morning the window near my bed gave me a glimpse of Japanese troops marching through Singapore. They were short, broad-chested men on muscular legs, in patched and faded uniforms, strutting behind the small rusty tanks that clattered through the street. It was five or six years since they had left their homes to fight a bitter campaign in China. Throughout these years they had lived hard, marching and fighting on meagre rations. Hardship had made them cruel. In Malaya (one of them told me later) they had bayoneted their own wounded and burnt their bodies; wounded prisoners had been thrown onto the fires alive. Now, re-equipped with British guns and stores, they were setting out to conquer Indonesia.

A week later I was sent, standing in the back of an open truck, to join the British prisoners-of-war at Changi, on the east coast of Singapore Island. I found the British officers of the Punjabi brigade living in a bungalow on the outskirts of the area. Behind the bungalow the ground rose to a small hill, crowned with an observation-post and a six-inch naval gun. The elder officers, sitting on a lawn or in the verandah, discussed the events of their brief campaign at bitter length. In front of them the Johore Strait was half a mile wide. Seen beyond the red flowers of the bougainvillias, the water was steel-grey in the early morning and at dusk; during most of the day it was a warm and rippling blue. An island lay in the strait, largely covered by trees, and beyond it the forests of the mainland stretched to east and to west. At first the prisoners-of-war were free to go fishing and bathing in the sea, but the few who tried to escape were caught and shot. One morning (perhaps as a warning to us) the Japanese brought seventy Chinese from Singapore city and shot them down on the beach with machine-guns. The bodies were left lying on the sand to be buried by the prisoners.

At the end of February, many of the Japanese troops were removed, and a new Japanese commander came in. The shore was put out of bounds, barbed-wire barriers sprang up and the prisoners were concentrated into smaller areas. Prisoners filled all the little Chinese houses of Changi village, through which a dusty road passed. The road was blocked at both ends of the village by a barbed-wire barrier; and halted here as they paced to and fro, the prisoners gazed over the wire at a hedge which had blossomed with the big pale-yellow flowers of alamanda. The officers of the Punjabi brigade now lived in a Chinese shop, a single room open to the street, in which they slept on the floor. The prisoners' diet consisted of rice (broken grains, mixed with weevils) of which we had enough for only one meal a day. Behind Changi street, the ground stretched level to a row of palm-trees which hid the seashore. Here we began to dig a waste plot with mattocks in order to grow vegetables for ourselves.

In April a thousand British prisoners were paraded in Changi street, to go as a working party to Singapore city. I went with them. They set off in good spirits, whistling and singing as they marched, but as the heat of the sun increased they trudged along in silence. In the afternoon they entered the city where their coming, made known in advance, was awaited by a large part of the population of Malays, Chinese and Tamils, who lined the pavements of the street. A number of Chinese women ran beside the column of prisoners, handing bottles of cool water to the thirsty men. Otherwise, a heavy stillness hung over the concourse. The prisoners, too, marched in silence; as they approached the city they had straggled, but now they closed their ranks and marched steadily, looking straight ahead. They passed through the city's streets and halted on the far side, while the day's heat faded in a drizzle of rain.

The men stood quietly under the trees while quarters were found for them in some empty houses that had been shelled in the last days of the battle. They entered in darkness and lay down on the floors, placing their haversacks as pillows. In the morning they were roused before daybreak and marched out to work, the sound of their feet dying away on the gravel. I was left alone with two sick men. I walked round the house and garden, where the lawn was littered with the wet ashes of a bonfire of books and papers. On three sides the garden was enclosed by spreading, rough-barked trees, whose little white flowers opened at dusk to give scent to the darkness for a single night; in the morning all the petals fell.

Once or twice I went with the men to their work and saw them digging the stiff clay, breaking stones and carrying the broken stones in baskets to construct a road. At an ornamental lakeside a group of Japanese carpenters in military breeches and puttees, but stripped from the waist upwards, were shaping lengths of timber for a bridge. Prisoners were driving wooden piles

24

into the water, working on a platform, which floated on three pontoons. Behind them the trees edged the water and were reflected in it. A temporary footbridge crossed the lake, formed of stakes and planks, lashed together. I held a sick parade in the evenings; soon fifty men were ill with malaria, dysentery and diseases of malnutrition. They lay on the bare floors of the empty house; those who were least ill nursed the others.

Sometimes the prisoners were roused for a midnight roll-call. Their feet stumbled on the road sleepily; some of the sick men dropped down on the roadside. The stars glittered above them, entangled in the boughs of the jacaranda trees. They stood in ranks while the Japanese counted them by torchlight. Always some men were missing; the Japanese grumbled and threatened to shoot them. But when the roll was called, all the names were answered, some by two or three voices. It was too dark to distinguish faces. The tired men stood shifting their weight from one foot to the other, and at length were allowed to return, trudging again up the hill beneath the hanging blossoms of the jacarandas.

A Tamil gardener, without work or apparent livelihood, had remained in the servants' quarters, close to the big house. He seldom showed himself, but one day, when nobody else was in sight, he asked me to come to see his child, who was ill with a fever. The entrance to his place was concealed by a trellis, overgrown with the leaves of a climbing-plant, perhaps a morning glory. The door was open; just inside, in a room which seemed dark to my eyes after the sunlight, a Tamil girl of about eleven years of age lay on a wooden bed. Her long hair was tossed back from her forehead over the pillow. I lifted her hand, feeling for the pulse at the narrow wrist. Although the room was cool, the skin was dry and hot. The child's eyes had a frightened look. After a few days, during which she grew better and at length smiled, I discontinued my visits. I saw that the Tamil gardener became uneasy when a Japanese soldier approached and saw us together.

A red, dusty road formed the rear boundary of the prisoners' area. I used sometimes to cross it quickly, to stand in the deep shade of the trees on the further side. The forest around me was silent except when the monkeys sprang noisily through the branches. Walking a short distance, I came to a clearing where a row of crosses, formed by the handles of bayonets driven point-downwards into the soil, marked the graves of British soldiers killed in action. At one side of the clearing a pile of burnt-out oil-drums stood rusting in the sunlight. Scraps of paper hung from some of the bayonets; stooping down to touch one, I read the name, 'Corpl. Cook, N. Norfolk Regt.' scribbled with a pencil.

On the far side of this forest-reserve I used to bathe in a pool. Once I came to a European house, which stood in a garden. I approached it across a

25

neglected lawn and looked in through an open window. My eyes met the gaze of a Japanese soldier who was seated at a table, eating rice from a bowl. The man's rifle was propped up beside him. I turned about and walked away slowly, forcing myself not to hurry, until I was hidden from the Japanese by a hedge. I thought he would at least halt me with a shout, but he let me go. His face had not been brutal; it was mild, friendly, interested.

When I returned to Changi I was sent to work in the barrack-hospital. In the wards the sick men lay idly on their blankets, tormented into irritability by the flies that settled on their skin. Their food was rice, of poor quality but now sufficient for two meals a day, supplemented with the spinach we grew on some waste ground. Sometimes a basket of fish was sent up from the harbour. The medical officers lived on the top floor of the building in a single large room where, instead of windows, wide glass doors opened into the balconies. The monsoon began with sudden gusts of wind, which rattled the doors and dislodged, perhaps, an enamelled mug or a shaving-mirror from its shelf. Looking out to sea, we saw the heavy clouds moving over the approaches to the harbour, but the squalls of rain were followed by sunshine. After supper some of the men pressed close to the single hurricane lamp and played cards. The majority sat in the shadows, talking in little groups.

In this dormitory I slept on a wooden door, unscrewed from its hinges and placed across two empty crates. My neighbour was a man called John Diver who, like me, had returned with a working party from Singapore. They had worked in the docks, he told me, and lived in a Chinese warehouse close to the harbour. 'The place was full of bed-bugs,' he added cheerfully: 'big, red, juicy ones!' He had the habit, when speaking, of pushing his cap over his fair hair to the back of his head. As a student living in London, he had sung in the London Bach Choir. He possessed a tattered copy of *Pride and Prejudice,* which he read repeatedly, often, at night, falling asleep over its pages.

He and I obtained permission from the Japanese to go outside the prisoners' area to gather firewood for the hospital kitchen. We went out in the evenings, passing a dismantled gun-position, already overgrown with climbing plants, and made our way through a deserted plantation to a creek. Here land and sea met around the hollow stems of the mangroves. We halted to watch the small, smoke-coloured fishes, which left the water and ran over the mud, using their fins as legs. 'I would give a lot,' Diver said thoughtfully, 'for the chance of dissecting one.' Our return-path took us through a coconut-grove, near a village of huts built on stakes and little platforms. We seldom saw the villagers, but one evening, between the trees, we caught sight of a group of young Malay girls, slender in the dusk, wearing the white, scented flowers of the champak in their hair. The girls scattered and faded among the tree-trunks.

26

An R.A.M.C. officer died at this time from dysentery. John Diver and I marched with the burial-party to the cemetery, which was in a clearing among the roadside trees. The soil thrown up over the recent graves was red; the green leaves around the clearing reflected the sunlight sharply. The mourners stood in ranks with their heads bowed while the chaplain read the service for the dead. The body, wrapped in rice-sacks, was raised gently from the ground and was lowered slowly into the grave. The corporal in charge of the burial-ground passed a handful of soil to the chaplain who, without interrupting the words, threw the soil into the grave. 'Forasmuch as it hath pleased Almighty God of his great mercy to take unto himself the soul of our dear brother here departed, we therefore commit his body to the ground; earth to earth, ashes to ashes, dust to dust; in sure and certain hope of the Resurrection to eternal life, through our Lord Jesus Christ.' A fatigue party on the road, wearing only shorts and boots, and pushing a load of firewood in a handcart, halted and stood to attention while the Last Post was sounded by a bugler. The bugle-notes died away, the fatigue party resumed their task, and the mourners dispersed from the graveside.

A Strange Journey

All night across the unseen plain
I travelled stiffly in the train.
At dawn beside the empty rail
I watched the morning stars grow pale.

The light with small successive shocks
Increased upon the tumbled rocks,
And soon a cactus, gaunt and dry,
Stood out against the reddening sky.

The birds were dumb, if birds there were;
No sound disturbed the steady air.
I looked around for track or guide
But nothing saw on any side,

Except, three furlongs to the south,
Outposts against the heat and drouth,
A group of trees. As near I came
A man's voice called to me by name.

A man I'd met somewhere before,
He stood beside his open door
And took me in. There quite alone
He lived beside his well of stone.

He said he had no food to sell,
But gave me water from his well;
And to my silent thought replied,
'Three years it is now since I died.

I knew that you would come this way,
And so I waited'. Who could say
How so strange a thing might end?
Was he my enemy or friend?

But soon he smiled and took my hand.
'I'll guide you through this quiet land',
He said. We went together then
To look for homes of other men.

5. North into Thailand

In the autumn of 1942 the Japanese began to take prisoners north to Thailand, to build a railway-line into Burma. When it was my turn to go, Diver gave me his own spare boots, as I had none. (I was wearing Malayan leather sandals.) 'You will need them,' he said; adding 'I expect I shall be following you before long. We must look out for each other when we get to Thailand.' But I never saw him again. A member of his party told me later, 'He saved many men's lives, but he never took much care of himself,' and he died in a forest camp somewhere near the border between Thailand and Burma.

We made the journey by rail, sitting on the floors of the railway-trucks on our kit. The train ran slowly and joltingly, while the sliding doors rattled loosely in the sides of the vans. Although a panel was left open for air, the smell of sweat and Malayan tobacco was strong. The seated prisoners were unable to stretch their legs, for they were huddled too closely; at night, half-asleep, their bodies swayed and lurched against each other. At intervals the train stopped, and a pail of cooked vegetables and rice was slapped onto the floor; and for a few minutes the men were allowed to walk off their stiffness at the side of the halted train.

The railway ran monotonously through forests, which pressed closely onto the track. The prisoners saw in the distance the summits of mountains turbaned in mist. They passed through Kuala Lumpur and crossed the Slim River at night, seeing neither. In the morning, at the harbour-town of Prai, opposite Penang Island, they watched the busy tugboats at work under Japanese flags. Further north they traversed a wide plain where the peasants were turning up the black soil in preparation for the rice-crop. At length, after three days and nights, their journey ended in Thailand, at a small town called Banpong. Here the wet ground of the transit-camp had been trampled into a paste of mud by the feet of the thousands of prisoners who had already passed through. The long huts of the camp were constructed of bamboo-poles and 'atap' palm-thatch; it was the pattern of most of the camps that we were to live in. The huts were open at each end; the floor was the bare earth. At this camp many of the prisoners bartered their shirts through the bamboo fence to the passing Thais for food.

Three days later a smaller party of prisoners, including myself, was sent up-country by river, the river Kwai-Noi. Before embarking, the men loaded the two barges, in which they were to travel, with rations for the Japanese troops. The path to the river ran by a crumbling wall of red brick and was overhung by palm leaves. An old woman with a wrinkled face sat in the shade of the wall and trees, with two children beside her, selling fruit from a large wicker basket. As they passed, carrying their loads, the prisoners made little jokes with the children, who soon jumped up and ran beside the men along the path to the river-bank, and held the men's hands as they returned.

Down Into Silence

The shoreward lights expired, their river-reflection
Faded; pleasure, care and desire
Grew dim and were drowned in sleep. The fire
Only of fireflies glimmered in any direction.

The barges waiting in the creek began
To move, and gained the ebbing river,
Silent, inert, except when a shiver
Of cold or fever seized and shook a man.

Within the hollow of their timbers
The captives (grey and shadowy ranks)
Sat close. The sliding river's banks
Were dark, lit by no dying embers.

What thoughts then occupied their minds?
Or had they gained or feigned indifference,
Imagination's farthest reference
Or empty rooms with lowered blinds?

Some men remembered children, wives,
And some, with or without contrition,
Errant loves, and some the attrition
Of mean and calculated lives.

But most (all who found any ease
Within the hold) slept in some fashion;
A handful only, freed from passion,
Looked up at the stars and were at peace.

In the late afternoon the barges were drawn out into the river by two tugs burning diesel-oil. The troubled surface of the water, carrying driftwood, flowed almost level with the river-banks, for the heavy rains of the monsoon had swollen its volume. At nightfall the prisoners and the Japanese guards went ashore; our cooks lighted a fire and began to simmer the rice. The light of the fire touched the hanging tips of bamboo-leaves and the roof-ridge of a nearby hut. A Japanese sentry came out from the shadows and ordered the cooks to smother their fire. 'I don't take orders from a Jap,' growled one of the cooks, a big, bearded Scotsman, and he threw another bamboo-log onto the flames. The next day the river-voyage was resumed, the men sitting cramped in the barges. A Japanese in one of the tugs fired his rifle at a party of monkeys, the sound of the shots echoing across the river from the forest on one side to the forest on the other. We were travelling upstream towards the mountains.

The next halt was made at another camp near the river, where the prisoners lay down to sleep on the ground beneath the overshadowing trees. At midnight a storm broke, the rain falling heavily for some hours. In the morning, when the sun came up, we lighted fires of brushwood to dry our blankets. Looking around me, I noticed that the forest was made up of three levels, the dry undergrowth, the thickets of bamboo, and the larger trees whose branches were spread as a canopy over the whole. The forest was almost silent, but when the wind pressed the tall bamboo-stems together they made a creaking sound. A yellow hibiscus and a mauve-coloured morning glory grew sparsely in the undergrowth.

At the end of the third day the tugs and barges drew up at a camp called Kinsaiok. Here the tired working parties of prisoners were returning from the forest. The men washed themselves at the river and ate their rice beside the camp-fires in the spaces between the huts. After supper I stood alone at the edge of the firelight. A man of about my own age came to me and said in a friendly tone, 'My name is Horne. We must try to make you feel at home here. I happen to be the camp-quartermaster. It doesn't make my job here any easier that the supplies of food are pretty short.' He told me the history of the eight hundred men who were already in the camp. They had marched to Kinsaiok from the base, taking three weeks over the journey, along forest-tracks made greasy by continuous rain. They had carried a month's rations on their shoulders. At one of the evening halts a drunken Japanese officer had run among the prisoners with his sword drawn, wounding one. Horne introduced me to the two medical officers, McPherson and Stone, who were already in the camp. McPherson had worked in Malaya for some years in a group of rubber-plantations, and he had a useful knowledge of tropical medicine. Stone had come from England only shortly before the capitulation of Singapore, and was younger.

Happy as Children

We marched; some had no boots and all
Were burdened. The road was dusty, hot.
The toiling guards soon ceased to bawl,
But carried rifles and would have shot.

We trudged in silence; the road was straight.
It rose and fell, the column too.
The sun opposed its burning weight,
And then a river came in view,

A wide, cool stream, unbridged, remote:
We halted at its sandy brim,
They signalled for a ferry-boat
And told us, curtly, we might swim.

31

How fresh the water was, how bright
The drops we splashed up in the air!
We raced and laughed in our delight,
Happy, without a thought or care.

When the camp fell silent I heard the sound of a waterfall and the hooting of owls beneath the cliff on the other side of the river. I found a place on the sleeping-platform of one of the huts and dropped my haversack and blanket there. In the morning, as a grey light entered the hut, I looked at the man who had slept next to me. The man's face was pale and the cheeks were hollow under the cheekbones. He said, 'I hope that you were not disturbed by my coughing during the night.' Later he told me that in 1940 he had gone with the expeditionary force that had been sent to Norway to oppose the German invasion. His platoon had been shot to pieces by the German tanks on the road north of Lillehammer. He himself had been wounded and was helped to escape over the mountains into Sweden by friendly Norwegians who had risked their own safety. After little more than another month in this camp in the forest he died (of lung tuberculosis) and was buried under the trees.

Inside the ragged thatch-walls of the hospital-hut, seventy or eighty men lay in rows on the bamboo slats that formed the sleeping-platforms on each side. The warm sunshine could not penetrate here, but a day-long twilight entered under the eaves. The two nursing-orderlies passed up and down, washing their patients in water, which was carried up from the river, and handing out the limited quinine. The sick men lay wrapped in their blankets, warm enough by day; but during the cooler darkness they shivered, and those who had the strength left the hut to sit close to the fires outside, which were kept burning until daylight. One of the sick men had a fishing-hook and line in his haversack and at nights he made his way down to the river-bank, where he sat fishing for some hours. Then, too weak to walk, he crawled on hands and knees back to the hut, after fastening his catch of fish round his waist with his fishing-line. The fish were roasted on spits at the fire.

It was little that a doctor could do here. To talk to a sick man, or to examine him, I had to climb onto the sleeping-platform and crouch there, first asking the man's neighbour to move a little. I spent many hours in this posture, judging that at least I could listen to the tale of the sick men's complaints and try to show some understanding. Under the conditions of forced labour and poor rations the sick-rate increased quickly, and the little cemetery beneath the trees had continually to be enlarged. The burial-squads entered at a stiff slow-march, the strips and tatters of their uniforms hanging from them.

32

The men's work lay in the forest, nearly a mile out from the camp. They marched away in the early morning, wearing shorts and wooden sandals, and carrying water-bottles, axes and tools for digging. The path crossed a stream and continued deviously between the clumps of tall bamboos. The big trees were felled and their roots grubbed up to make way for the railway track, which was planned to pass up into the mountains between Thailand and Burma. When the bridge across the stream was half swept away by floods, some convalescent sick men were sent out to repair it, using timber that they cut as they needed it. Horne and I went with them and stood waist-deep in the water, driving stakes into the pebbly bed of the stream. On the second day, when the work was finished, we lay on the ground to rest before returning to the camp. A man with a whimsical look on his face approached us.

'This is better than home,' he said. 'Here I work only twelve hours a day; at home I work fifteen.'

'Who do you work for?' asked Horne.

'For my old mother, sir; she keeps a little fried-fish shop in Hoxton. Of course,' he added, 'the grub was better at Mum's.'

The prisoners who went out to work were paid ten cents a day, the price of an egg. The sick men were paid nothing.

Sometimes a trading-raft was brought up the river and was made fast to the bank opposite the camp. Twice a day one of the Thais from the raft, most often a woman, paddled a canoe across the river to sell eggs and bananas and little rice-cakes to the prisoners. She came to a point below the Japanese landing-place, out of sight of the Japanese sentries, where the bank was steep. Here the canoe floated, a black streak on a disc of sunlight beneath the trees. The woman crouched in the stern, with her paddle beside her, and smiled as the men scrambled awkwardly down the slope.

I had experienced my first bout of malaria soon after reaching the camp, feeling the symptoms that were to become so familiar, the headache, the shivering, the prostration, the reviving sense of warmth. My second attack came on Christmas Eve; by the end of the afternoon I could stay on my feet no longer and was glad to be stretched on the ground in our tent (our hut was not yet completed). In the evening the Japanese gave permission for the prisoners to have a concert. From where I lay I could see the great bonfire under the trees and the heads and shoulders of the men outlined against it. The smoke flew upwards, and the trunks of the trees reflected a rosy shimmer. I heard the songs and the sudden shouts of laughter. Nakao, a Japanese soldier, came into the tent where I lay.

'Nakao,' I said, 'I am Iyoki.' (The word means sick).

'I am sorry,' said Nakao, squatting beside me. Before the war he had been a student at the University of Tokyo; his father had lived in London for a while and worked for the Yokohama Bank. Nakao had some painful sores on his hands, and came to McPherson to have them dressed. The Japanese army, he told us, had little medical organisation. He himself belonged to the Corps of Engineers.

It was a strange Christmas that followed. In the early hours of the morning a blurred moonlight filtered through the mist. The moisture settled on spiders' webs and dropped from the pendant leaves of bamboos. The vapour hid the hillsides, so that when we emerged from our huts and tents for the morning roll-call, there was no indication of any world beyond the mist, except that we heard the sad wailing of the monkeys. The Japanese commandant had allowed us to keep Christmas as a rest day (the first since the camp opened). We fetched our rice without haste and ate it with a sense of ease. A major of the East Surrey Regiment came to the hospital-hut and read the church service. Later, the mist cleared, and the blue sky was seen with the burning sun high up in it. The men moved about the camp idly; some retained an appearance of health but many were bony and wasted. They took their clothes to the river and washed them, standing naked. Afterwards they swam, splashing and shouting and forgetting their hardships. The sick men lay resting in their huts. The medical officers held their sick parades, dressing the jungle-sores on the men's legs and admitting the fresh cases of malaria to the hospital.

The Japanese commandant of the camp had been (he told us) a lawyer in civilian life. He had planned the construction of the camp himself, opening up the forest so as to gain a view of the mountains. In the evenings he put on a kimono of white bath-towel material and sat in his hut. He could be seen, for the atap wall ceased halfway up to the roof and a polished lamp hung above his head, which was bare and close-cropped. At first he had business with his subordinates, who came and went. Then he sat alone, upright, staring out into the night. Sometimes he gave a tug at his moustache, sometimes he lifted a glass to his mouth. A pot of cold tea stood on the table in front of him, with a bottle of brandy beside it. He smoked one cigarette after another. He was uneasy about the state of his prisoners. 'You English are no good,' he grumbled, 'why must you die?'

In the New Year of 1943 this commandant was recalled to Banpong, and was replaced by a lieutenant who had orders to press on with the work more rigorously. The Korean troops in charge of the prisoners became more truculent. They were stocky men, broad in the chest, with short legs and peasant faces; oppressed themselves by the Japanese, they enjoyed their authority over the prisoners-of-war. I saw one of them beating a man outside the hospital-hut, hitting him about the head and legs with a stick. I had to intervene, and the Korean walked away grumbling, but I did not like this sort of incident. Many of the less seriously ill men were sent out to work. An

34

additional task was to build new huts for three thousand Dutch prisoners-of-war, who were expected from Java. Soon they began to arrive in the camp, travelling in lorries, six hundred at a time. The majority were Javanese half-castes, speaking Dutch, who had never seen Europe. But some were highly-cultured men. One said to me, 'It is valuable to be able to think oneself away from this camp.' He spoke of an international exhibition at San Francisco, where he had designed the Netherlands-Indies pavilion. He died some months later, leaving me the poorer from the loss of a friend.

I met one of his countrymen later who had been glad of his opportunities for finding flint arrowheads and other Neolithic tools while working on the railroad near Chungkai. But many of the Dutch were anxious about the wives and children whom they had left behind in Java and Sumatra under the harsh conditions of the Japanese occupation.

It was now the dry season. The doctors' small hut was overhung by a tree, eighty or a hundred feet high, with a rugged bark. Its great leaves, untidy and dry, fell slowly. Then, when the tree was bare, its angular twigs broke into blossom and soon a shower of yellow petals floated down. I shared this hut, which stood close to the hospital, with McPherson and Stone, the other medical officers. In it we had constructed two beds, a narrow table and a bench, all of bamboo. McPherson, who came from Glasgow and had a sea-going ancestry, could use his hands and a simple knife to good purpose. Stone slept on a low camp bed, beneath which he stored a few eggs and onions, and a little jar of coarse brown sugar. One evening I sat reading at the table by the light of a cotton rag floating in diesel-oil. I had borrowed a small Bible from McPherson. 'I have never read it through myself,' he said, 'but I hope to have time for it now.' I read the words, 'A certain Samaritan, as he journeyed, came where he was, and when he saw him, he had compassion on him and he went to him.' I paused here, as I heard a quiet tap on the doorpost, followed by Horne's voice, 'May I come in?'

'Come in,' I said gladly. The hut had no door.

'What are you reading?' Horne asked.

I read aloud, 'A certain Samaritan, as he journeyed, came where he was, and when he saw him, he had compassion on him and went to him.'

Horne said, 'That is what some of the men in this camp are doing all the time, aren't they? Both out at work on the road and in the camp here. A sick man is always helped by the men on either side of him.'

Horne, serving in an R.A.S.C. unit, was an engineer by profession. He told me that at the age of fifteen he had been sent by his father to work at a foundry in Pittsburgh, for his father wanted to broaden his mind and to give him a good practical education. He had been a shy youngster, he said, and he still remembered with gratitude the kindness of the elderly foundryman and

35

his wife with whom he had lodged. He spoke of his own wife with a quiet affection. They lived in London and were, to his regret, childless.

One evening as I sat alone in the hut after a visit from Horne, I took a scrap of paper from my haversack, removed the cork from my little bottle of ink and wrote:

> Now from the tropical trees,
> Helga, the leaves fall
> Slowly, singly. A mist creeps
> Cold over all.
>
> Sick in their narrow huts,
> Men droop and die.
> Released by death, beneath
> These trees they lie.
>
> Helga, in this sad place
> Where sorrows kill
> My hopes, I find your face
> Dear to me still!

This name was often in my thoughts but I did not speak of her.

As time went on, I fell ill with a form of dysentery. One day as I was recovering, I walked slowly along a path into the forest, rustling the dry leaves under my feet. When I had gone less than a mile, I dropped onto the ground and lay prone, my eyes shut, my head resting on my arms. My body was glad of the warmth that it took from the soil. When I looked up, I saw between myself and the trees on the further side of the clearing a cloud, or moving skein, of yellow butterflies, falling and rising in the air as they flitted over a stream. Sad as I was, I felt an impulse of joy seep and flow through me. I watched the butterflies until they flew out of the glade, then I rose and made my way back to the camp slowly.

So we came to the middle of March, and past the middle of the dry season. The noonday heat was intense. The trees of the forest were bare, but soon they began to blossom, and in places they perfumed the forest paths.

6. Interlude: At Kinsaiok

At Kinsaiok, half a mile above the camp, a waterfall on the hillside dropped from the edge of the forest into a basin of rock and from there it swirled downwards into the river. The place was visited by few of the prisoners, and often I sat alone on the smooth, sun-warmed rock, scarcely listening to the thunder of falling water, or heeding its spray. Here I was able to forget the prison camp; the uneven, sun-baked ground inside the palisade, the untidy huts with their roofs of palm-thatch, the tired working-parties; and the rows of sick men with their hollow, bearded cheeks, lying inert on the bamboo slats. I watched the vivid flight of the bee-eaters as they pursued insects over the river and heard the little snap of their bills. Sometimes a Thai barge travelled beneath me, strongly built of thick timbers and given a hooded appearance by its rounded roof. These boats passed out of sight beyond the bend of the river, but they carried my thoughts far in distance and time, to the scenes of my early childhood; for I was born in China, in the province of Fukien, whose main highway of travel was the River Min. I had journeyed with my parents in similar boats and I remembered their smoky interiors and the smell of the boatmen's cooking. Our home was at Kien-ming, a city surrounded by a high wall of stone, into whose crevices the small grasses had thrust their roots. I remembered the yearly Feast of Lanterns, when the rigid shapes of fishes and dragons were carried on poles through the dim streets, with candles burning inside their bamboo-ribbed bellies. We lived, however, outside the city's gates at the mission-hospital where my father worked as a surgeon.

My father left China on furlough, taking his family with him, in the old P. & O. ship, *Marmora*. One evening, as we entered the Straits of Messina, my father carried me up from the cabin in his arms, to point to Mount Etna, rising from a calm sea and licking with little tongues of flame the violet sky above. Arrived in London, my parents took lodgings in Canonbury Square, in Islington, in order to live near my mother's parents. The tall windows looked down onto the gravelled paths of the Square, bordered by laurel-shrubs. In those days the traffic that jolted along the sides of the Square was mostly horse-drawn. It was here that I first saw falling snowflakes, as I knelt on a chair and pressed my face to the window-pane. In the room behind me my mother bathed her baby in front of the fire. It must, I think, have been a Sunday evening, for after the baby was left sleeping, my mother taught my sister and myself the children's hymn,

> There is a green hill far away,
> Without a city-wall,
> Where the dear Lord was crucified,
> Who died to save us all.

37

An old journalist who reported Parliamentary Debates, and lived above us, sometimes came banging noisily downstairs, demanding that the brats should be silent. The sound of his fist on our door frightened me, but on other occasions, as we met him going in or out of the house, he was gentle and gave us picture-postcards with views of foreign cities.

My parents returned to China soon after my sixth birthday; my sister was younger. We were left together at a boarding school in the country. In the winter evenings the children crowded round the black iron stove, but in the summer, in the hay-making season, they played in the long swathes of mown grass. We spent the holidays with our Islington grandparents, who lived in a grey Victorian terrace-house with a long garden behind it. My sister wore a navy-blue jersey and little skirt; her face was shaded from the sun by a wide-brimmed sailor-hat. She busied herself with her dolls and her toy-pram, while I played with a wooden horse and cart; or we scrambled along the garden-wall, looking for spiders in the ivy. In the middle of the morning my grandmother came out and sat, grey-haired but upright, in the shade of a pear-tree, with a colander on her lap, shelling peas. The long forenoon ended when we heard a voice calling from the direction of the house, 'Come in, children, and wash your hands.' Looking up, we saw one of our aunts standing in the verandah, in front of a French window, with the shadow of a wisteria falling across her face. On winter evenings, as we lay in bed, we could hear the newsboys crying out in the street below, their voices piercing the soft rain and the fog. The motor-buses wheezed by, and bars of light swung across the ceiling as they passed the shuttered blinds of our window.

This was in 1914, when the First World War began. The following year our nights were disturbed by Zeppelin-raids and by the gunfire that accompanied them. We were roused from sleep to sit downstairs in the basement kitchen for safety; looking at the ashes in the grate and hearing sleepily the purring of the cat, which slept in comfort on the cook's lap. The cook was a middle-aged, kindly woman from Suffolk, who seemed to have a particular fondness for cats and children.

My father and mother returned to England, bringing two younger children. We lived at first in a farmhouse in Surrey, now the site of Gatwick airport. At six o'clock in the morning the sun was shining brightly on the scrubbed boards of my bedroom-floor. No one else in the house was awake. I went quietly down the back stairs, lifted the scullery latch and stepped out into the sunlight. The copse at the rear of the house was floored with bluebells. Daniel, the lame boy who worked at the farm, was milking the cows in the long, whitewashed shed. He hobbled from stall to stall, the milk spurted into his pail, and the cows were turned out into the yard. There was a smell of straw and manure; a heap of mangolds lay against a wall. When Daniel had poured the milk into the big churns, he harnessed the pony to the cart and drove off to the railway-station. To me it seemed a long time to wait until breakfast. I sauntered into the copse to cut myself a stick, and spent a half-hour notching it with my pocket-knife.

The date was early in 1916; my father had come home from China in order to join the army, in which he served as a surgeon. My mother was left single-handed with the children (as many women were left at that time). In later days I remarked to her, 'It must have been a hard time for you,' and I reminded her of an evening when we had broken a treasured Chinese vase in our play, and when later, coming downstairs, I heard her crying behind the closed door as she picked up the fragments. She said that she had forgotten this incident, although she admitted the loneliness of those years. But it is a happy time for a mother, she added, when her children are small and are dependent on her.

As a boy at boarding school, I was a good deal away from home, but when, in 1924, I became a student, my father had settled in medical practice in Stoke Newington, in North London, and I could live beneath his roof. He had borrowed the greater part of the money he needed to buy his house and the practice, and until he had repaid the loan he felt obliged to live stringently. Unless the weather was bad I walked daily to the medical school of St Bartholomew's Hospital, in Smithfield, and walked home again later, in order to save the bus-fares. In this way I gained some familiarity with the streets and the street life of Clerkenwell and Islington, but I took no part in the social life of my fellow-students, and made only a few friends. The house to which my father had moved was of a Queen Anne date. We spent the winter evenings upstairs. My sisters sat at the table over their school homework. My mother sewed, making and mending clothes. She managed somehow to help a number of humble friends, sailors out of a job or charwomen too old to work, who came in the evenings to the side-door of the house. My father was busy below us; occasionally we heard his voice as he conducted a patient out of his consulting-room. Later in the evenings I sometimes went out and walked through the dark streets before going to bed. Here and there, in the springtime, a laburnum or a lilac-tree drooped its flowers over the wall of a garden and caught the lamplight.

At St Bartholomew's I began to work in the Casualty Department, and then in the hospital wards. Our clinical teacher had a curious, quick way of speaking, and the habit of repeating a phrase. 'Look at your patient, look at your patient,' he would say, standing at the foot of the patient's bed and addressing the students around him. We looked at the patient and saw the propped shoulders, the skin pallid except for the flushed cheeks, the pointed nose and the nostrils moving with each quick intake of breath. What thoughts passed through the brain behind the alert, uneasy eyes we were never invited to consider. The long ward, with its polished wooden floor, received the sunlight from the big sash-windows opening onto the square outside. Here, in the evenings, the plane trees sheltered a vast number of starlings which settled, whistling and preening themselves, among the branches.

Once I went for a holiday in Cornwall on my bicycle. I watched an old farmer drive slowly down a country lane, holding his pony back with the reins; the wheels of the trap grated on the flints of the road. His wife was seated beside him, clasping a basket in her arms and swaying with the jerky motion of their vehicle. At the bottom of the hill its wheels splashed through the water of a ford, overhung with ripening elderberries. A dog came out from a farmyard and barked at them. Half-hidden by the trees, the tower of a little church rose from a graveyard, overgrown with nettles. Within, the sunlight barely penetrated beneath the rounded stone arches. On Sunday the candles had flickered on the altar. The priest had mounted the pulpit and read aloud the sad words of Martha and Mary, addressed to Christ, 'Lord, if thou hadst been here, my brother had not died.' This was true, he said, spiritually and also of wars. The war of 1914 (in which three of my uncles were killed) was still in our minds.

I rose to my feet from the sun-warmed rock and, leaving the waterfall, I made my way back to the camp; to the hospital-hut and the suffering men there. As I went, I passed close to the forest clearing where we had buried our fellow-prisoners as they died. The space was very quiet. On many of the grey tree-trunks surrounding it some of our Dutch friends from Java had grafted the tropical orchids that they had found growing on trees elsewhere in the forest. The pure colour of the flowers, shaded and almost hidden, seemed to express something of our love and grief for the dead and offered a haunting suggestion of eternal beauty and peace in some far-off paradisal Galilee.

7. Hindati

In March two hundred of the healthier men from Kinsaiok were chosen to move to a new camp, further up the River Kwai-noi and nearer the mountains of Burma. They started early, while the morning was still cool, each of the men carrying his pack or haversack, his blanket and his water-bottle. The kerosene-tins, which were used as cooking-pots, were slung on a pole between two men. The column marched struggling through the forest, sometimes mounting onto higher ground, sometimes dropping into a hollow. At the rear of the column a Japanese soldier marched alone, armed with rifle and bayonet. At dusk we entered a camp of Dutch prisoners near the river; a burial-party was moving out, bearing three stretchers covered with rice-sacks. On the second day of the march the forest became thinner, and at sunset we reached our destination.

The new camp, known as Hindati, lay in a depression formed by a swamp; it was not far from the river, by which supplies were still brought up on barges from Banpong. At this time of the year the swamp was dry and the rushes had been cut. The prisoners slept in some rows of threadbare tents. In the sick-tents, under my care, the sick men lay on split bamboos on the ground. Every morning the Japanese sergeant, or 'gunso', came to inspect the sick men and to pick out those he thought fit for work. Every morning I protested. 'These men are all ill,' I said; 'they cannot work.' The gunso looked with bloodshot eyes first at me and then at the sick men; he put his hand on his sword-hilt threateningly and jerked his head as a signal for the sick men to follow him.

In the forest a wide corridor had been cut through the trees; the undergrowth had withered, and the trees had a bare, tormented look. The sunlight beat on the naked shoulders of the men as they swung their picks and mattocks, and carried the soil in baskets to build a raised embankment. They worked in silence, the stronger helping the weaker; a sick man's work was done by the men on either side of him. The Japanese shouted orders. Sometimes a sick man was brought back to the camp. I would look up and see two prisoners in ragged shorts, carrying a third man between them as they descended the slope. They laid the sick man on the bamboo slats, placing his haversack under his head and making him as comfortable as they could.

The Japanese administrative office was a long hut of bamboo and thatch, standing on the higher ground above the camp. The building, pale brown in colour, was overhung by the heavy green leaves of a giant forest tree. At the foot of the tree a captive monkey ran to and fro, jerked suddenly backwards by the rope which was tied round its neck. Inside the hut the light seemed to be faintly green; three clerks, seated at a table, bowed their heads over strips of paper inked with neat figures. The two gunsos, or staff sergeants, had their own desks. From time to time I was summoned for an interview with the medical gunso. The interpreter was a Dutchman from Java, meagre in his threadbare uniform, with a thin beard. The gunso asked,

'Why do your patients die of malaria? Do you give them quinine?'

'I have not got enough quinine,' I said, standing in front of his desk.

'I have given you sufficient,' said the gunso, whose name was Matsuoka, 'you must not waste it.'

In April the weather changed. Every evening a thunderstorm broke and beat down the cooks' fires. The lower end of the camp became a shallow lake,

41

through which the returning working parties splashed as they went to the river to wash themselves. The grass and rushes began to grow again and were soon head-high. In the evening flocks of small brown birds rose from the reed-beds and rushed through the air on rapid wings, rising and falling and settling again.

At the end of April and during the first half of May the forest road that linked the camps was traversed by many thousands of prisoners, Dutch and British, who were sent to complete the railway nearer Burma. Some jolted dustily in lorries; others marched, stepping aside among the trees to allow the lorries to pass. Each night a new marching-party stopped at the tents by our stream and sent to us for their rations. Among them were some officers of the Punjabi brigade with whom I had come to Singapore; others, they told me, had been left sick at Kanburi and Tarsao, and one had died. I walked out to their tents after supper and talked with them. We sat under the trees by a fire, which they had made to keep off the mosquitoes, and they gave me scraps of news from the outer world, which they had picked up. The Russians were fighting at Stalingrad, the Americans in the Pacific. Another evening, in similar circumstances, I talked with a passing M.O. Looking round at the troops under his care, 'I used to think,' he said, 'that most of us would get out of here alive, but now I am beginning to doubt it.' The sick men of the marching parties were left under my care at Hindati. Later on, some thousands of Tamils, coolies from the plantations of Malaya, were brought up; and many hundreds of them died of dysentery, cholera and malnutrition.

In order to gain some shade we moved the sick men's tents under the fringe of the jungle, on the higher ground. Here they lay in the gloom, listening to the splash of the rain on the leaves and to the drone of the mosquitoes. The two nursing-orderlies, Sgt Barry and Pte Montiero, both Eurasians, worked unceasingly, tending the sick men with gentleness and concern, always cheerful and willing. I had another attack of malaria myself. Then McPherson came up from Kinsaiok and took over my responsibilities for a few days. Leslie Horne came also, and resumed the habit of joining me in the evenings. As we sat talking on a log of wood outside the tent, he seemed quieter than before. He spoke of the men whom we had left behind at Kinsaiok, describing their sufferings, which in many cases had ended in death. If ever he reached home himself, he said, he had many messages to carry to their families. He was memorising the names and addresses, in case the Japanese should deprive him of his notes.

When the work at Hindati was finished, the working parties were sent deeper into the forest, staying out for days, and then for weeks at a time. They built bridges over gullies and streams, using the forest-timber that they felled. They slept in the open, beneath the trees, lying on the ground. McPherson, now himself looking thin and worn, went with them to care for their sick. I remained at the camp at Hindati. When told by the gunso one afternoon to expect some sick men who were coming in, I walked out into the forest to meet them. The forest-path was sunny, but the men who came towards me had an earthy look. The first was a tall, gaunt man, leaning with both his hands on a long stake. Behind him, two men clung together, but it was difficult to say which supported the other. The rest followed; some had puffy faces and swollen legs, others were so wasted that the skin seemed to be drawn tightly over their bones. Horne and McPherson came last, shoving at the hand-cart which carried the men's haversacks and blankets. 'God help you,' said McPherson as he handed them over to me, 'most of these men are almost dead already.'

I led them to a frayed and leaking tent, where they stretched themselves on the ground. But the same evening the medical gunso, Matsuoka, came to pick the men for the next day's work. He sat on a bench beneath a tree while the sick men filed in front of him. Standing at his back in the dusk, I saw the outline of his round head and I promised myself that if ever I got the chance to hit that hard skull I would smash it. 'These men are all ill,' I said angrily, 'they cannot work.'

'Be quiet, the gunso shouted, 'or I will send you into the forest to take their place.'

'Send me,' I said, 'I want to go.'

'You don't know what you are talking about,' growled the gunso. But the following morning the sick men remained in their tents, and the gunso did not show himself again for three days.

The rain fell heavily and almost continuously. The swamp in which the camp lay became a mire. All the tents were moved onto the higher ground at the edge of the forest. Here the rain dripped from the trees onto the canvas, and leaked and trickled down the thin material. The men lay on the bamboo slats, irritably shaking off the mosquitoes, which whined all the time in their ears and settled on their skins. They were nursed, day and night, by the two nursing-orderlies, who brought them their meagre rations and helped them onto the makeshift bamboo bedpans. A Japanese medical officer came to inspect them. They were forced to their feet and came out into the clearing, where they formed a ring round the doctor. At his command they turned and broke into a run, but they could scarcely lift their feet from the ground and soon fell exhausted. Barry and Montiero picked them up gently, almost tenderly, and carried them back to their tents.

Cholera had started among the prisoners in a camp higher up the river. As a precaution the river at Hindati was placed out of bounds. The prisoners were told to wash themselves in a pool below the Japanese cookhouse, into

43

which the cookhouse rubbish was thrown. Sometimes in their hunger they were glad to seize and gnaw a piece of vegetable or other garbage that floated in the water. Ten days after the Japanese doctor's inspection, and as a result of his report, the gunso told me that all the sick men in the forest were to be sent downstream to a hospital-camp at the base. The next evening the sick men at Hindati were carried to the river-bank and were loaded onto two barges. The river was in flood and the boats rode high on the water.

I was left lonely in a mood of depression. The gunso said to me, 'Tomorrow another barge will come, and I will send you downstream too.'

'I would prefer to stay here,' I said. 'Don't be a fool,' said the gunso, 'you are ill.' The gunso, a broad, clumsily-built man, stood scowling at me and grumbling, but I knew that in his morose way Matsuoka was trying to befriend me.

Marching through the Forest

Innocent and happy days,
Lambs lying in the meadow,
White blossom blowing from the hedge,
The future free from shadow:

I lost it all. My spinning world
Has reached another climate,
Broad forests brooding in the sun,
Where each man's grief is private.

We marched beneath the hanging boughs,
And every rank was broken;
We shared the heat and heaviness
But seldom words were spoken.

At evening to the river-side
The women come for water.
The dark-skinned boys are bathing, and
The banks resound their laughter.

8. Back to Kinsaiok and Tarsao

The river was again swollen by the rain; the barge was fastened with difficulty and swung on its ropes. It was empty except for the Thai boatman and a single Japanese soldier. The Japanese was a big, dark-skinned man, who had a quiet, thoughtful look. When the voyage began he seated himself on his kit and looked across the swirling water to the trees of the river-bank. I walked down the length of the barge, beneath the cowled roof, stepping carefully from one to another of the great wooden baulks of its hull. Travelling up-country nine months ago, I was one of the many prisoners who had sat, cramped and pressed together, in the barge. Now I was alone, and I wondered how many of my previous companions were still alive.

Kinsaiok, too, had changed. The camp to which Horne had welcomed me had gone, replaced by a larger and sadder-looking area of human effort and suffering. New huts had been built, pushing the forest back in all directions, but the older part of the camp was in a state of decay and the newer huts, put up hurriedly, also had a tumbledown look. My Japanese guard led me up the path to the local gunso's office. The gunso searched my kit roughly; apart from my blanket it was all contained in a single haversack, but I also carried a pack. 'What is in this?' asked the gunso.

'A dozen tins of condensed milk,' I said, 'which the medical gunso at Hindati told me to give to the English doctor here for the sick men.'

'I will take them,' said the Kinsaiok gunso briefly.

'But the medical gunso at Hindati told me to give them to the English doctor.'

'I will take them,' the gunso repeated. 'I need milk also.'

I was sent to sleep behind the Japanese guard-room, in a lean-to shed. Here I found a young officer of the Argylls, named Primrose. He was under guard by a Japanese soldier, with whom, however, he seemed to be on friendly terms. He was tall and broad-shouldered, and stood leaning against a doorpost. 'What are you doing here?' I asked him.

'They are sending me to Bangkok for trial,' he said. He told me that a sick man had come to Kinsaiok from one of the up-river camps. It was soon clear that his illness was cholera, and in order to prevent the spread of the infection the Japanese commandant had decided that he should be shot. A squad of Japanese soldiers had lined up to fire from a distance at the little tent in which the sick man lay alone, because they were afraid to go nearer. 'He might have been hit half a dozen times,' said Primrose, 'without being killed.' He had taken a rifle from one of the Japanese soldiers and gone into the hut. Beneath the hot canvas the sick man lay on the ground, already unconscious; the flies were crawling over his half-closed eyes and over his excreta. Primrose put the

45

muzzle of the rifle to his chest and pulled the trigger.

As I entered the hut Primrose had been talking to the Japanese soldier who stood leaning on his rifle, with a grin on his broad face. 'This fellow is teaching me Japanese,' Primrose explained, 'and he is laughing at my mistakes. When I was a lad at school in Campbelltown, they said I would never learn anything, but they were wrong, because I am now learning to speak Japanese.' He turned and spoke a few words to his guard, who grinned more broadly and replied in his own language.

I continued my journey to Tarsao by barge and again climbed the river-bank. Tarsao was now the rail-head. The forest had been widely cleared and the bare ground had been churned into humps and ridges by the wheels of lorries. The long train was waiting in a siding; it consisted of goods-trucks only, some of them open, some covered. The Japanese soldier who was with me entered a covered truck, after directing me to climb into an open one. Two hours later the train began its journey. At first I stood up, holding the low side of the truck with my hands, and watching, mile after mile, the trees of the forest slip by me. When the sun went down the air became cold, and I lay on the floor of the truck. A storm woke me, the rain drenching me in a moment. I could see nothing in the darkness. I crept to a corner of the truck, hoping for some shelter, but the rain streamed down my back and limbs, and I was shaken by the movements of the train. The thunder rolled overhead. I began to shiver as an attack of malaria took hold of me. My head ached and throbbed. In my fever I remembered a phrase from the Bible, 'the deep darkness where God was,' and I tried to creep close to my Creator in the tumult of the storm.

The train stopped in the dusk of dawn in some paddy fields, and I heard the Japanese soldier calling my name. I rose stiffly, swung my legs over the side of the truck and jumped, my feet splashing water upwards as I dropped. The Japanese went ahead, trailing his rifle. I slung my haversack loosely over my shoulder and followed.

At first the unfinished huts, the stacks of atap-thatch and the scattered poles of bamboo offered the prisoners little more comfort than the forest camps. The convalescent sick men used to sit on the ground inside the fence, looking across a plain to a road, where small buses and pedestrians moved against a background of casuarina-trees and white villas. A tall chimney stood beside a factory and formed a subject for conversation day after day, the men calculating and arguing its height and diameter; there seemed little else to talk about. They washed themselves in the flood-water behind the cookhouse. Beyond the huts in that direction the camp ended in some neglected paddy fields, where a Japanese sentry in a patched uniform stood on a dyke. Here, while attempting a walk, I was stopped by a blow on the head from the

46

sentry's fist and was ordered back to the huts.

The new parties of sick men from up country arrived in the evenings. Always they had lost one or two on the journey; a barge leaked and a sick man was drowned in the bilge-water; another fell over the side, the barge being crowded, and was unable to swim. Or they died in the trucks of the train. They came into the camp after dark and were unloaded from the lorries that brought them by the light of hurricane lamps. They were ragged and dirty; some of them walked on the bare bones of their feet, from which the flesh had rotted. When the sleeping-platforms were full, they were placed on the mud floors to wait patiently for better accommodation.

In the long hut where I lived I had been allowed to build a screen of thatch to separate my bed from the rest of the sleeping-platform. Among the cobwebs beneath my bunk a little white she-cat, which had strayed into the camp, gave birth to four kittens. Each night, before sleeping, I lowered my lamp into the corner where the kittens lay peacefully, seeing perhaps a tiny paw outlined against the mother's milky fur. Sometimes I was joined by Read, the senior medical officer in the camp. Read was often, however, occupied until late in the other huts, dressing the ulcers on a sick man's legs, a task which he liked to do himself. Two English prisoners lay on the other side of my screen, out of sight but not out of my hearing. Read came in one night and sat on my bed. 'I met a girl in Brighton,' said one of the two voices on the other side of the partition; 'I picked her up on the seafront.' Read heard the man's story in silence; then he looked at me and shrugged his shoulders; he was a broadly-built man, deliberate in his movements. 'I had to sack those two men from the cookhouse,' he commented. 'They came and asked me for a job there, but I found they were pinching the sick men's food, so I sacked them.' Read had served in France in the early part of the war. 'The Germans didn't have it all their own way in 1940,' he said. He had been able to buy extra rations for the sick men with money given to him by a Chinese merchant living in the town near-by.

Read had gone out of the camp a number of times at night, climbing the fence, and made his way in the dark to the merchant's house. 'I went myself,' he told me, 'because I did not like to ask anyone else to take the risk.' He had also obtained a stock of sulphonamide tablets, which he asked me to hide in the hollow bamboo struts of my bed. Later, when I left the camp, I took the tablets to Read. 'Keep them,' he said, 'you will find them useful where you are going.' But I refused. I knew that I was likely to be searched at the guardroom as I left. I knew, too, that in another part of this camp three officers had been beaten to death with leather belts by Japanese soldiers, because they had operated a wireless receiving-set. It lay in the bottom of a kerosene-tin in the cookhouse, covered by a layer of peanuts. The hut was searched and nothing

47

was found, but as the Japanese soldiers turned to go, the tip of a bayonet-scabbard accidentally struck the tin and knocked it over, exposing the wireless-set at the bottom.

One evening Gus Ward came into the camp with a party of sick men from the railroad. He had been our adjutant at Hindati; and as such had received the orders for each day's work from the Japanese. Before the war he was a tea-planter in Assam, and I have no doubt that he was a kindly employer. I found him on the sleeping-platform of one of the huts, eating his rice in the dusk. He called out my name as I was passing; I hung my lantern on one of the bamboo poles and sat down beside him. He had suffered many attacks of malaria. He told me that the railway-track had been completed by the working parties from Burma meeting those in Thailand in the region of the Three Pagoda Pass. Sergeant Jago was dead, he told me. I remembered him as a lively, fair-haired young artilleryman. 'His leg was injured at work,' Gus said. 'They were hauling a log up onto a scaffolding. "The knot's no good," our men said, "the rope is slipping." The Japs shouted and told them to pull. The log fell, crushing Jago's thigh. He marched back to camp somehow and went out again the next day, but he had to be carried back at night. The leg swelled enormously and got horribly painful. Doc Stone operated and let out three pints of pus from the thigh. Then it swelled below the knee; Doc Stone operated again; he did his best, he had only an old razor-blade to work with.' Gus himself had become ill again and was left behind at a Dutch camp where conditions were even worse than at Hindati.

In November Horne arrived with a party of sick men. He was himself weak from malaria and spent most of these evenings with me. 'I have never,' he said once, 'seen a Japanese show any pity, for the sufferings of these men. That is why, in my own mind, I had condemned them. But, coming down here in the boat, I had a talk with one of the Japs and I began to understand. Most of them were born in the slums of Tokyo or some other big city, and their homes were desperately poor. They have served overseas in China and Malaya for five or six years, and have lived like homeless dogs. Many of their comrades are dead. Perhaps always, if you know enough about people, you can find something to pity; and pity is halfway to liking.'

Horne went on, 'There is plenty of courage in this world. What is needed is more compassion and understanding.' The other men in the hut were now asleep. Horne and I moved outside and stood looking silently at the stars. The long shadows of the huts lay around us, indistinct in the darkness, with brooding ridge-poles and thatch. Only in one of the huts the light of a hurricane-lamp moved slowly as Read continued his rounds, dressing the sores of the sick men.

This renewal of our friendship lasted only for three weeks, for towards the end of the month both Horne and Ward were transferred to the original base-hospital at Kanburi. Shortly afterwards, Gus Ward sent me a note by a man who went out of the camp with a working party. 'Our friend Leslie Horne is seriously ill with cerebral malaria, and has been unconscious for two days.' Two days later I received a further note, to the effect that Horne had died. He was buried by a small, sad party of his friends, who carried his body out of the camp to the prisoners' cemetery. When, later, I visited this burial-ground I could not identify his grave; children and dogs scuffled about in the dust, but the graves were nameless.

In the quiet afternoons, awaiting the return of the working parties, Read used to sit outside the hut, mending his clothes. 'This reminds me,' he said once, 'of a sunny window-seat at home where my mother used to sit to darn our socks when we were children.' A short distance away the little white cat lay on the ground, blinking her eyes at the sun and watching her kittens. A Japanese sentry paused on his rounds and stood looking down at them, resting his weight on his rifle-butt. The flies drowsed on a wall. Time moved slowly in this camp.

In the New Year of 1944 some of the prisoners were moved again, and I was included among them.

9. To Nom Pladok

We travelled to Nom Pladok by rail. Standing in the open trucks, we saw ahead of us the sinuous length of the train running between dry paddy fields of a general tawny colour. The crops were cut, and the families of peasants winnowing the grain rested at noon under the squat trees. The women and girls waved their hands at the passing trainload of prisoners. Nom Pladok was a bare expanse of brown dust enclosed by a bamboo fence. It was a new camp in which the British formed the minority, and the administration was mainly Dutch. The Japanese commandant was the lieutenant whom we had known and disliked at Kinsaiok. The camp contained five thousand men who had been invalided from the Burma railroad, many of them still seriously ill.

The Japanese appointed me as senior medical officer, although most of the Dutch doctors were older and more experienced. 'But that is as it should be,' said the oldest, stroking his beard, 'the English are good administrators.' The Dutch adjutant did not agree. After bribing the administrative gunso, Takashima, with the gift of a gold ring, he had been able to purchase some medical supplies which he made his excuse for interfering with my work. He quarrelled also with the friendly Dutch doctors, whom I found to be excellent

49

colleagues. But, to be fair to him, he worked effectively to keep the camp clean and in good order.

The camp hospital consisted of five huts, long and narrow, each holding three hundred and fifty men. The low sleeping-platform ran the length of either side; the central gangway was straddled by the poles that supported the roof. Roof and walls were made of atap palm-thatch, the floor was of dried mud. I had the care of two huts, with seven hundred sick men. I was happy when one day McPherson walked into the camp with a party of men from Hindati and was able to take over some of my work. It was good, too, when Gus Ward came from Nom Pladok and was put in control of our cookhouse, where there had been some unhappy disputes about the rations.

A hut for patients with dysentery stood slightly apart from the others. Here the sick men lay on the ground. It was easier, then, to lift them onto the bedpans, made of wide split-bamboos. The nursing-orderlies had insufficient water for washing their own hands, and they had no disinfectants. The flies crawled over the bedpans and over the wasted bodies of the sick men. The nursing-orderlies who worked in this hut were all volunteers. One, a Dutch naval officer, fell sick himself and died.

He was buried by a Dutch protestant padre who was in the camp. He stood in his rumpled green uniform, with the tears running down his cheeks as he spoke from the text, 'Greater love hath no man than this, that he lay down his life for his friends'. As the senior medical officer I had to make a daily report to the Japanese headquarters, the usual thatched hut on bamboo supports. At the entrance I bowed (as required) to the Japanese officer who sat at his desk, before approaching the medical gunso or his clerk. Sometimes I was punished for the failure of hospital-patients to comply with Japanese orders, or for protesting against orders that were unreasonable. One day, when I had reported a death, the medical gunso said, 'You must make a post mortem examination, to see whether it was amoebic or bacillary dysentery which caused this death.'

'The illness was like bacillary dysentery,' I said; 'I have no instruments for making an examination.' The gunso, Matsuoka, handed me a long pointed knife.

'You must make the post mortem examination,' he insisted, 'it is an order from Tokyo.'

I found the body lying on the ground and I knelt beside it. A little daylight entered through the door of the hut and through the gap beneath the thatch-roof. I lifted the rice-sack that covered the body and made a long incision with the knife. When I had finished I rose to my feet, but I looked again at the pale, drawn face, and I knelt again beside the dead man. I had known him in one of the forest-camps, and I recalled now that he had been a coal-miner. I saw in my imagination a grey village on a moor, a narrow street of stone terrace-houses and in the background a great heap of slag cast out from a pit. Perhaps he had a wife and children who were still hoping for his safe return from the war.

It was now the dry season; the camp was bare of grass and shade. The wells were half-empty, and water was scarce. In the evenings, when the huts were dark, I walked to and fro inside the boundary-fence, where my feet had worn a path in the dust. Beyond the fence I saw the wasteland which had once been rice-fields; a few stunted acacia-trees bordered a road. I watched the movement of the wind over the dry, brown grass from which, during the day, sometimes a skylark flew up, singing.

One afternoon in the wet season that followed, a sudden storm came on. I hurried to the nearest shelter, a small disused hut, built for medical stores which had never arrived in the camp. I halted at the entrance beneath the dripping thatch, for I heard inside the hut a voice reading aloud in English. I looked in and saw a small group of men seated on the earth-floor of the hut, facing the reader, who, with his back propped against a post, was carefully scanning the open pages of a Bible. He was an older man than the others, slightly bald and wearing tarnished steel spectacles; and he read in the hesitant, awkwardly-phrased way of a man with little education. He was reading from one of St Paul's epistles, 'Who shall separate us from the love of Christ? Shall tribulation, or anguish, or persecution, or famine, or nakedness, or peril?'

In this camp the time passed very slowly. Nothing distinguished one day from another. At the morning roll-call I stood with the sick men. The dawns were cool, and some of the sick men shivered slightly in their rags. Beyond the fence the sun disentangled itself from the trees. Its rays were at first almost parallel with the ground, and the shadows of the ants crawling over the dust were distorted. After the roll-call the working-parties formed up and were led away. The sanitation squads went to work about the camp. The nursing-orderlies began the daily care of the sick men. In the cookhouse the rice was put to simmer in the big stew-pans. In the hot afternoon the wind rose, driving eddies of dust across the camp.

One morning some hundreds of prisoners were sent to the river, to return with a load of bamboo-poles and thatch for enlarging the camp, and I went with them. The morning was fresh and clear after rain. From a mud embankment we saw the curve of the river and a white sail. A dozen barges were drawn up against the bank and were in process of being unloaded by bare-footed Thai women, wearing full, dark-blue skirts. The lank, bony prisoners moved stiffly about their tasks. They said nothing, but perhaps they watched with pleasure the plump, lithe girls as they ran up the gangways and swung their loads onto their shoulders. Behind them, on the road near the river, a Buddhist funeral-procession went by, led by the yellow-robed monks, with a tinkling dirge of music. A similar cortège was sent to the river for several days, and sufficient building material was brought back to enlarge the camp to take another two thousand sick prisoners from the up-river camps. But at the end of May three thousand prisoners, Dutch and British, were sent from Nom Pladok to Singapore, and from there they were shipped to Japan.

One evening the Dutch interpreter came to my hut. 'The medical gunso, Matsuoka, wants to see you,' he said. I followed the young Dutchman across the camp. The gunso's hut, built of the usual bamboos and thatch, was small and sparsely furnished; it was lit by a hurricane lamp hanging from a rafter. The gunso, Matsuoka, sat at a small table. 'You have been wasting the medical supplies,' he said. I had heard this complaint often before.

'No,' I said, repeating the routine denial, 'you give me very little.'

'You must not be wasteful,' said the gunso, frowning. He looked up at me. 'I want to talk with you,' he said, and for the first time in all our meetings, he added, 'Sit down.' He nodded at the narrow bed, made of split bamboo and covered with a thin mat; a blanket lay rolled at one end. I sat down on the bed. The gunso's right hand, resting on the table, tapped his pencil for a few moments. Then he asked, 'Why are you English fighting this war?' I had almost forgotten its origins.

'To defend our country,' I said.

The gunso grunted. 'You talk of freedom, don't you? I don't wish for anything except to serve Japan. Nothing can stop the Japanese army from ruling all south-east Asia and India. You understand that?' Then, with a gloomy look, he went on, 'But the war does not go well for us at present.' After a pause he added, 'You must not forget. The Japanese never surrender.' In the event he refused, in the only way open to him, to participate in the Japanese defeat.

※

The evenings, month after month, were passed in the monotony of talk. Men sat in groups inside the huts, clustered around the little oil-lamps, which the ingenuity of some had devised. Here all topics were discussed, from the deeply personal to the general. Looking out from the dark interior, I saw the moonlight whitening the thatch of the neighbouring huts. The open space between the huts was blotched with groups of men, squatting or sitting on the ground. Some of the prisoners paced up and down slowly. It was an hour of relaxation. Perhaps a third of the men were Europeans: the remainder, although speaking Dutch, had an ancestry going back to the coasts and hills of

Indonesia. I thought with curiosity of the personal past, known only to himself, which lay behind each of these men. The last bugle was sounded at eleven; after this the camp became still, except for the slouching march of the Korean sentries.

Since our first coming to Nom Pladok, whenever the moon was full, we had heard the engines of R.A.F. reconnaissance planes and bombers passing overhead at nights. Their droning vibration filled the air, drawing near and then sounding directly above us. The Korean guards shouted, running about the camp. The sound died away, to be followed by distant explosions in the direction of Bangkok. As time went on the bombers came more often, and flew lower. The Japanese mounted some anti-aircraft guns behind our cookhouse. One night in early September the moon was full. We heard the planes approach and soon, looking out from our huts, we saw them clearly in the moonlight. When they returned the Japanese guns opened fire. We lay on our beds, the air throbbing around us as the shells screamed over our heads. Two of the planes replied with their machine-guns, uttering a defiant note. After they had gone we heard the crying of plovers, disturbed in their marsh.

The Japanese had decided to close this camp and accordingly they gave orders that the sick men were to be moved to a neighbouring camp, half a mile away. The sick men now numbered less than seven hundred; most of them were able to walk, shouldering their kit, and the remainder were carried on litters. The whole formed, with their Japanese guards, a long, straggling procession. The medical staff accompanied them.

The new camp, known to us as Nom Pladok I, was situated in an area of railway-sidings and workshops, which provided work for many of the prisoners. Trainloads of Japanese troops and war-material passed by every day, and the noise of shunting went on late into the night. The camp was congested, for its area was small and the huts were placed close together; in each of the huts the prisoners lay shoulder to shoulder as they slept. Here I renewed acquaintance with Dobson, whom I had known slightly in the early period of our captivity in Singapore. It appeared that his parents and mine were neighbours at home, and I had seen him one Christmas with a party of children, making a snowman in the garden of his parents' house.

I was happy to see him again. We met outside our hut in the evening after my arrival, and we stood talking for perhaps half an hour. When we separated it was a clear, starlight night. The moon, two days past its full, had not yet risen. I lay down to sleep on the floor. I was wakened suddenly by the thud of bombs bursting a mile away. A moment later the bombs were falling in the camp. When they stopped I ran outside the hut. The moon rode high overhead, and in its light I saw dusty men lying on the ground; none seemed to move. The ridge of a nearby hut had a curious twist in its length, and cries of pain could be heard from inside. Then I saw the lanky figure of Dobson, running. Catching sight of me, 'I'm afraid you are wanted over there,' he said quietly. 'Some of my men have been hit.' Some, indeed, were badly wounded; two lay dead, side by side; a third body was huddled under the short steps of the hut. The whole camp was now astir. Half a mile away a large fire was burning at a petrol-store, and a vast column of smoke, streaked by the flames, was swelling upwards into the sky. We worked by its light, removing the dead and wounded from the stricken huts. No slit trenches had been dug in the camp (the Japanese had not allowed it), so the men had been lying crowded together on the sleeping-platforms. The wounded men were carried into a large hut which was untouched; the dead were laid in rows outside on the ground. The administrative gunso, Takashima, came and looked at the bodies; he refused permission to light lamps in the hospital-hut, and indeed we had no adequate lamps, so the wounded men lay in darkness until the morning. Some died, no doubt, who might have been saved. No Japanese were hurt, and the Korean guards had found safety by running into the neighbouring paddy fields.

At daylight the medical staff set to work; we operated all day, stripped to the waist and using with our bare hands what instruments we had. The medical gunso gave us morphia and bandages. A hundred and fifty men had been wounded; of these twenty-three died later; seventy-two had been killed outright. In the late afternoon a long funeral-procession left the camp; the bodies, wrapped in rice-sacks, were carried on improvised stretchers. The next day, when a Japanese staff-officer arrived from Bangkok, most of the wreckage had been cleared away. The wounded men lay in rows on the floor, with clean dressings and bandages, but some had lost an arm or a leg. The Japanese colonel spoke a little English. 'The bombers will come again,' he said.

He was right, for this raid proved to be the first of a general attack by the R.A.F. on the whole Thai-Burma railway. In reply to this threat the Japanese began to move parties of British prisoners into maintenance-camps along its course. Three hundred men were to be sent from Nom Pladok under Dobson's charge, and I asked to be allowed to go with them. The party left Nom Pladok on the 13th September. We stood waiting in the rain for two hours before starting. Friends who had come to say goodbye turned away and went back to their huts. A little Korean soldier, who had a wrinkled, shrivelled-looking face, came to me and handed me a parcel containing eight hard-boiled eggs, a present for the journey. He was a man whom I had known slightly in more than one camp, without ever learning his name. He smiled, but said nothing.

10. Up Country and Back

I was glad to be going up country again, after fifteen months in the base-camps. The train ran for some hours over a level, cultivated landscape; when it entered the forest it began to climb. Over-shadowed by the trees, small groups of prisoners waved from the maintenance-camps along the line. The men in the open trucks of the train replied cheerfully. Night came, and the engine, burning wood for fuel, puffed fiery sparks into the darkness. At a midnight halt a voice cried from one of the trucks, 'What place is this?' Nothing could be seen below the sides of the train, but a second voice replied briefly, 'Harrow-on-the-Hill, mate.' A gust of laughter shook the prisoners.

The next day they marched by a jungle-path from the railroad to a hillock above the river. A half-built hut was seen in a clearing. The men began at once to make a camp, enlarging the open space and cutting poles of bamboos for the huts. The next morning they started work on building a bridge to cross the river, here seventy yards wide. A pile-driver hammered the posts with a rhythmical thump, its weight alternately raised and let drop by the effort of forty men in two floating pontoons, who strained at the long ropes. The river swirled past them. The forest-trees rose massively on either side of the river, their tallest trunks providing material for the bridge. On the sloping banks blue-and-copper-tinted butterflies flickered above the green patches of amaranth.

A Japanese corporal, or 'heicho', was in charge of the camp. Every evening he came to the hut to give instructions for the next day's work. 'Sit down, Johnny,' said Sergeant Parsons, inviting the heicho to climb onto the sleeping-platform, where he sat cross-legged. A candle was planted on an upturned box between them. Dobson, the senior British officer, stood looking down; he was a tall man, his face dim in the darkness above the candlelight. A lance corporal of the East Surrey Regiment stood at his elbow as interpreter. When the men of the working party began to sicken with malaria, I reported them as unfit for work. 'You are a very bad doctor,' the heicho grumbled, 'these men are only pretending.'

'Our doctor knows better than you,' said Dobson obstinately. Fires were kept burning outside the huts to frighten off wild animals, but at the first sound of R.A.F. engines the Japanese sentries ran out, shouting orders to darken the camp. But the moon shone still, and the bamboo leaves at the edge of the clearing caught its light and sent it cascading onto the dark humus beneath. The prisoners, too, came out of the huts and stood listening, while the throbbing engines filled the night with their sound.

The first stage of the work was finished when all the piles for the bridge were driven and stood in ranks across the river. The sun had shone

55

unremittingly all the long morning, and all the long afternoons, while the men worked. The river flowed beneath them, with its eddies glistening. Its surface was brown, reflecting little of the green vegetation on its banks. Here the trees rose sixty or eighty feet in height before spreading out into a shady mass of foliage. The heicho had promised a rest-day when the bridge was completed; and in preparation for the holiday I went with our canteen-officer in search of extra provisions. We walked by a forest-track for four or five miles and came to the river-bank opposite a small town called Takanon; we crossed the river in a hired canoe. The town appeared sleepy in the early afternoon, although we were told that it served the needs of the workers in a nearby tin-mine. It consisted of two unpaved streets; two children were playing in a runnel of water that crossed one of them. A boy who was lame dragged himself along on a single crutch. The shops were little more than booths open to the street. We entered the largest. The shopkeeper was friendly; he had travelled as far as Singapore, and spoke English. He took us into an inner part of the shop, lighted by a naked electric bulb hanging from a wire; and making us sit down at a small table, he brought us two cups of coffee. He was ready to supply us with all we asked for, on credit, and promised to deliver to us two sacks of dried peas (known as 'kachang idjoe'), some native brown sugar (gula malacon) and a quantity of ducks' eggs. He brought them by river-launch the next day, unloading them at a point on the river-bank, half a mile above the camp.

When the bridge was completed a working party was sent to repair a road through the forest on the far side of the river, and a detachment was sent further upstream to build a second bridge. The remaining officers lived together at one end of the long hut; there were three of them, apart from myself. One evening they sat talking by the fire of sticks that burned at the entrance to the hut. I had gone to bed early with a headache. But I was unable to sleep; the drawling voices of my companions disturbed me. 'Why can't you stop talking and let me sleep?' I cried irritably.

'Don't be a fool,' said Dobson, 'we shall talk all night if we want to.'

The next day my headache grew worse, and I lay helpless, sweating and shivering. I felt ashamed of my ill-temper of the previous evening. Dobson, who had the next place to mine on the sleeping-platform, brought me water to drink and to wash with, and climbed with his long legs onto the bamboo slats to make me as comfortable as he could.

My other neighbour on the sleeping-platform was Primrose, whom I had first met in the guardroom at Hindati. 'How did you get on at Bangkok?' I asked him.

'All right,' he replied. 'After the trial the Japanese colonel who presided came to my cell. "You are a free man," he said. I was not altogether free, but he took me for a drive round the city in his own car and gave me a good meal.'

Primrose went out every day with the working parties; even now he was stronger than most men. One evening as he and I stood near the Japanese cookhouse, a prisoner brought in a load of firewood for the cook. The fastening slipped and the load of wood fell off the man's shoulders. The Japanese cook swore at him. The prisoner turned away sullenly. 'You can pick it up yourself,' he said. The Japanese pulled out his bayonet with a threatening look. In a moment Primrose stepped up to him and gripped him by both his arms; the Japanese was unable to move. Primrose spoke to him slowly, quietly, good-humouredly, in his own language, the Japanese of a city slum. The soldier listened in surprise and then burst into laughter, lowering the sharp point of his bayonet. Primrose picked up the load of firewood himself and carried it into the cookhouse.

When the fever had passed I walked down to the river-bank to wash the sweat off my skin. I saw the forest, the strip of yellow sand and the far-off mountains in the evening light. As I returned to the clearing where the huts stood, I heard in the stillness the drone of an engine. I stopped and stood still, scanning the sky until I saw in the distance an aeroplane above a gap between the high hills. It drew nearer, and was followed by two more. All three planes swung over our camp, seeming to darken the sky with their wings. Our sick men had been hastily carried out of their huts and placed in a ditch, but the R.A.F. had bigger objectives. They swept down the length of the Thai-Burma railway, their bombs crashing into the bridges and smashing them. This was the first of the daylight raids.

Behind the clearing in which our camp had been built an old road entered the forest. Everywhere it was much overgrown and because it was shady it was the haunt of many birds. It seemed to invite me to an exploration of the forest, and one day I determined to follow it. My feet made no sound on its surface. The path led away from the river, winding among the trees. Where it crossed the open track of the railroad I hesitated, and then I stepped over quickly. The path climbed, a stream gushed through the undergrowth, and a flock of red-billed starlings flew from the summit of a glossy peepul-tree. The path curved and crossed the railway again, and here I saluted the Japanese soldiers in charge of a small repair-gang. I was allowed to pass without question. Next, I met two British prisoners collecting firewood, who told me that they came from a small camp nearby. A few minutes later I entered a clearing where, beneath the trees, two lines of huts faced each other. Underneath their bedraggled thatch a few prisoners-of-war lay sick. They told me that their doctor was himself ill in the far hut. 'May I come in?' I asked, and, entering, I found inside my old companion from Kinsaiok and Hindati, McPherson. He

57

lay on a bamboo frame on his back, his thin arms resting on the threadbare blanket which was drawn over him.

'I am glad to see you,' he said. 'I wish I could give you a better welcome.' He smiled apologetically at the mud floor, the bamboo table, the rusty enamelled mug. 'You have come just at the right time,' he went on. 'I have been unable to go out and see my sick men today. I would be grateful if you would do this for me. Are you still interested in birds? This is a wonderful place for orioles.' I had already heard them calling to each other as I entered the glade.

'Do you remember Deighton?' McPherson asked me, 'he was with us at Hindati and afterwards. He died here recently.' Horne had already told me about this man. He had been a member of a small working party that moved from place to place, bridging some of the smaller streams in the forest. Once, when they shifted camp, a number of sick men were left behind, unable to march, and Deighton stayed with them. He cooked their food, washed them and nursed them; finally, as they died, he buried them. When the last was dead, Deighton rolled up his blanket and rejoined his working party. His home, Horne told me, had been among the poorest streets of Manchester.

'You must come again,' said McPherson. 'I have a pocket chess-set and I would like to give you a game.' Before leaving this camp I walked down to the river and bathed. I swam upstream and downstream, enjoying the soft touch of the water. When I had finished I lay down on the clean sand, allowing the warmth of the sun to dry my body.

In our own camp the sick-rate was rising inevitably as the result of our continued exposure to malaria. I had with me Sergeant Barry, one of the two medical orderlies at Hindati, who, on hearing that I was going up country again, asked to be sent with me. He brought along another good orderly, named Nichols. In December we suffered our first death, a young lance corporal of the Royal Northumberland Fusiliers. But our employment was coming to an end; the bridges were finished, the forest-road was repaired. Tasks were found for the men, but they were not urgent. Our little community seemed isolated; in our clearing the huts of bamboo and thatch were dwarfed by the massive trunks and foliage of the trees. Our knoll above the river shrank in comparison with the great hills that limited our perspectives. The hilltops themselves were hidden by mists almost until midday.

Then the Japanese told us that we would soon be returning to Nom Pladok. 'The work is finished,' they said.

※

It was the middle of January, 1945, when we started on the return journey to Nom Pladok, leaving the jungle-camp empty. Nearly half the men were ill with malaria. We marched in a narrow column along the path between the dry trees. The sun shone; the dead leaves rustled under the tread of our feet. I noticed that a man ahead of me was swaying on his legs as he marched. The two men beside him quietly took his blanket and pack, and carried them. We climbed into a train at dusk, and sat huddled together on the floors of the trucks, the more fortunate propping themselves against the sides. We travelled only at night, passing the days idly under the trees beside the line. On the second night the train halted in a cutting for some hours, while British bombers flew above us in the darkness. On the third night we detrained at Nom Pladok, at a siding that had been bombed. The tall tops of coconut palms could be seen against the night sky above the wrecked railway-carriages, which lay gashed and twisted on their sides. The stars stood still above them. One man of our party, who had been carried unconscious for most of the day, died soon after our arrival.

Since the last air-raid the prisoners' camp had been shifted slightly away from the railway-lines; and the huts nearest to the railway had been abandoned. The camp-area was brown, dry and dusty; the slit trenches (which the Japanese had at length permitted) zigzagged across it like a queer sort of maze. Only a few trees, a species called *Sesbania albiflora*, lent some grace to the scene; they had a dainty, slender beauty, their blossoms resembling small white ships in a sea of green foliage. Air-raid alarms had become frequent, both by night and by day. The important bridge at Rajburi, fifteen miles away, was bombed twice in the darkness by the light of flares which were dropped from the bombers. The prisoners waited beside the slit trenches with their blankets drawn over their shoulders, while far-off in the sky the flares budded and opened and sank slowly. Once, a bomber force of more than sixty planes passed over us in a slow and impressive pageant. Flying at perhaps twenty thousand feet in the blue tropical sky, they were quite silent, for at such a distance the sound of their engines was lost before it could reach us.

But this camp at Nom Pladok was a dreary place, and I was glad when after only a month we were told that we were to be moved again.

11. Final Journey: Ubol

The final journey was to the north-east of Thailand, to a town called Ubol, near the border with Cambodia. The prisoners set out again by rail, after waiting at the side of the track while a battalion of Japanese troops marched down the road from their transit-camps. The Japanese were short, stumpy men in threadbare uniforms, bent under the weight of their loads and leading a few shaggy ponies attached to small field-guns. They occupied the front part of the train, while the prisoners scrambled into the cattle-trucks at the rear. The first break in the journey was at the bridge of Nacomchase, which crossed a moderate-sized river. Its three central spans had been smashed by bombs and had been replaced by a swaying improvisation of bamboos. We crossed slowly on foot. In front of me a blind Dutch-man was guided by one of the Korean guards. From this point we continued the journey in a second train, which carried us slowly across the level coastal plain, cultivated as rice-fields but now dry and bare. Isolated farmsteads stood under the shelter of a few trees. The late afternoon saw our arrival on the river-bank opposite Bangkok, the capital city of Thailand.

We left the train and waited outside the station, which was close to the river. At six o'clock a number of barges drew in to the river-bank; the prisoners were taken on board and were packed beneath the rounded awnings, where the space was dark, hot and airless. I contrived to go on last and was left standing outside the hold in the well of the barge, from which I looked out across the broad current of the river. Japanese soldiers were despatched to find a tug, and later, when the tug and its owners had been found, there was a further search for petrol and oil. As darkness fell, the mosquitoes settled on us, piercing the bare skin of necks, backs and limbs. On the far side of the river the lights shone out from the great buildings, and were reflected from the water; later, as we continued to wait, the lights were extinguished one by one. The river became misty.

My thoughts travelled back to London, where in the dusk of a November afternoon I had first seen a Norwegian girl, named Helga. She was lodging in a quiet square in South Kensington, in a house with a grey-plastered front, whose lowest windows were in part hidden by laurel shrubs. As I descended the stairs, following the quick steps of a child, I caught sight of Helga through a doorway. She stood alone by a fireplace with her head bent, her fair hair touching a shoulder, one hand resting on the mantelpiece. Instead of leaving the house, as I had intended, I turned abruptly into the room. Helga raised her eyes with a smile as the little girl pronounced my name. Behind her a bowl of flowers, white, red and bronze chrysanthemums, glowed on a table; the heavy green curtains were drawn across the window. It was her first visit to

London, she said, and everyone had been very kind to her. I asked myself tenderly, how could anyone wish to be unkind to her? We remained standing, for our talk lasted only a few minutes. Before turning to go, I asked if I might come to see her again. As I walked away through the darkening streets her image met me in the misty air, whichever way I looked, elating me. And again I saw her now, with hopeless longing, in the miasma of Bangkok.

At midnight the barges in which we sat began to move downstream, roped together and following a diesel-launch. The launch was silent, for the current of the river carried us; only some ripples disturbed the water. The shores of the river were invisible. As the boats passed beneath the arches of a bridge, partially destroyed by bombs, its central cantilever was raised high above them, like an arm in awkward blessing. The prisoners sat humped on the floorboards, their heads drooping on their chests, dumb and drowsy in their tiredness. How many, I questioned, could entertain dreams that lightened their darkness? Or were they bowed and bent down by their sorrows and regrets? Or had they learnt by long endurance to feel nothing?

The next three nights we slept on the concrete floor of a warehouse, adjacent to the wharf and the waterfront. Far away to the west, the sun sank behind low palm-trees after throwing a crimson glow across the water. When an air-raid began the prisoners were allowed to run fifty yards along a road and tumble into a trench dug at the roadside. Here, in the darkness, they watched the red flames rising into the sky above the city. At Bangkok we entrained again.

After travelling all night, the train halted in the freshness of dawn and the prisoners were permitted to climb down; they did so stiffly. A few Thai villagers, clustered beneath a palm-tree, shouted, 'The war will soon be finished!' and were dispersed angrily by the Japanese guards. We had reached a high, barren plateau. There seemed to be nothing between the train and an indistinct line of hills except a giant cactus, shaped like an upright cross, which grew boldly from some rocks in the centre of the plain. At the dawn of the second day we reached the bank of a great river, which, after being allowed to bathe, we crossed in shallow pontoons. We marched through the streets of a little town and for the last eight miles of the journey we straggled as an uneven column of men along a straight and dusty road. Both the guards and the prisoners were tired; the Japanese shouted irritably and the prisoners replied by swearing sulkily.

The gunso, Matsuoka, marched beside the column of prisoners. He stared ahead as he marched, but seemed to see nothing. His short, thick legs, in their darned cotton breeches, moved stumbling, for the roadside was uneven. Perhaps by choice he kept abreast of me, but he did not speak. From time to time he raised a hand and brushed his fist across his eyes, as if to dash a harsh

61

or threatening thought from his brain. Then he resumed his plodding march, withdrawn in his silence. He never made the return journey along this road, for when the Japanese defeat seemed inevitable he shot himself with his revolver. On hearing this news, I felt a strange regret.

The site selected for the new camp was an area of dry and disused paddy fields, but the camp buildings were not yet in existence. The earlier Dutch parties of prisoners had been given bamboo and atap-thatch to construct small shelters for themselves. The later arrivals lay on the open ground, because the supply of building-materials had failed. A working party of five or six hundred men marched out of the camp every morning to build an aerodrome. Their work consisted of carrying basket-loads of rubble for the construction of a runway; it was a monotonous task, in which they were exposed all day to the blistering sun; and they had to march the seven miles home again in the evening. They seldom returned to the camp before dark, and sometimes they were delayed until midnight. In March further runways were constructed near our camp. Occasionally a British reconnaissance plane flew overhead as they worked.

We had no certain news of the outer world, but we could see that strange things were happening around us in Thailand. The three contingents of prisoners-of-war, which should have followed us from Nom Pladok, had failed to arrive. An explanation was provided by the Japanese quartermaster. 'We may find it difficult to get rice for you,' he said, 'because the R.A.F. have bombed the railway between here and Bangkok.' In the new camp the work of building proceeded slowly. Bamboo and thatch were scarce because the Thais were unwilling to sell materials to the Japanese for their paper money. The local population showed an increasing hostility; and the Japanese soldiers became reluctant to leave the camp after dark. The Japanese commandant built his house within the stockade, to protect himself from attack. The day-to-day administration was in the hands of the gunso, Takashima. He was arrogant, dandified and ill-mannered. He searched our kits repeatedly. Those of us who wanted to keep anything personal found concealment increasingly difficult. I stitched a small wad of thin notepaper, comprising some account of our captivity, into the soles of an old pair of leather sandals, which lay worn out in my haversack. But the gunso was understood to have admitted that the war in Europe was nearly finished. 'The news is very bad for us,' he added. A rumour went round the camp that the Americans had landed in Saigon.

But gradually the material was bought, and the barrack-huts were built within the stockade. The prisoners moved into them, about three thousand in number, of whom only the working parties ever went outside the camp. In the long sick-hut the men lay on slats of bamboo, with eyelids closed. Some, indeed, had lost their sight as a result of malnutrition, and needed to be led by the hand when they left the sleeping-platforms.

It was at about this time that the Japanese shot a young Australian who had been caught outside the palisade of the camp at night.

⁂

There is little more to be told of the months that we passed at Ubol. In spite of our crowded quarters it was a lonely time. Most of the people with whom I shared rations and sleeping-quarters were companions of necessity. Sometimes, in the evenings, men of the working parties whom I had known up country came and told me of little events which had occurred outside the camp. They were still employed on the runways and landing-strips of the aerodrome, but the Japanese seemed to have lost heart. Few aircraft made any use of the place, whose construction was probably part of an old plan which had lost its meaning as the war-situation changed. Our camp was completed with stockade, ditch and rampart; we had never before been so enclosed. Machine-gun posts were also constructed but the Japanese never found any weapons to place in them. Regrettably, disputes arose in the cookhouse between the Dutch and British cooks about the rations. Cormac, my neighbour on the sleeping-platform, was appointed as mediator. He was a kindly, genial man, able to listen patiently to both sides of an argument, nodding his head as he did so. He was also a good doctor; and in difficult cases I was glad to rely on his judgment.

Mimosas at Dawn

The flowers which all night through appear
To float, each flower a little sphere,
Amongst the leaves, at dawn reveal
The stems which stars and clouds conceal.

The light which breaks across the hills
Pervades the outer leaves and fills
The inner space; each shady bay
Receives its dim, retarded ray.

Puffed milky orbs, borne high or low,
The flowers reflect the morning's glow.
The leafy stems, affirmed in light,
Will hold their burdens now till night.

⁂

63

One night the heavy rains of the monsoon began. Lying awake on our bamboo-slats, we heard the raindrops tapping steadily on the roof and splashing from the thatch into the gutters below; in the drainage-channels of the camp the water ran gurgling. By morning the level area of the camp and the surrounding countryside was under water; only the great mounds built up by the white ants and the low embankments of the rice-fields stood out from the inundation. The date was about the middle of June.

In Thailand it seemed that there was an internal migration of birds, related to the rains. As the dry season advanced the birds left the forests and the open country, and flocked to the rivers and marshes. Later, when the rains came and the land became green again, the birds dispersed and spread themselves once more over the countryside. So, at this time, our camp was visited by larks, pipits, flycatchers, orioles and hoopoes. The ioras, whose yellow breasts and black tails could be seen from below, were constant singers in the trees. Ron Scrafton, one of the men from the working parties, used to come and tell me of the birds he had seen outside the camp. He had worked as a foundry-man in Doncaster before the war, and he told me that he had been interested in birds since childhood. As a soldier he served in the Royal Corps of Signals. After the rains, when the small white flowers and reddish leaves of the sundews (*drosera*) could be seen on the moist, sandy soil, he was at once interested in their insect-catching habit.

Birds in a Quiet Place

This forest-clearing, planted
With a peasant's simple crops,
Is now deserted.
The ground was left to lapse

To stillness. The brinjals, shedding
On the path their unpicked fruits,
Are linked to spreading
Bindweeds and bamboo-shoots.

The parakeets fly clamant,
But soon the field reverts
To stillness, patterned
With delicate notes of birds.

The delicate notes drop tinkling
Among the verdant leaves,
Cool like that sprinkling
Of dry, neglected sheaves.

The Methodist chaplain in the camp was also a North-countryman. He held his services out-of-doors in the evenings, after the men returned from their work. The cicadas dinned in the trees until sunset; when the sun went down they became silent, and the crickets began to chirrup in their burrows in the soil. I was glad to kneel sometimes with these ragged prisoners who had suffered so much. The padre recalled them with directness and simplicity to Christ's Sermon on the Mount; to the birds who 'sow not, neither reap nor gather into barns', and to the lilies whose glory was greater than Solomon's. He was not ignorant, however, of modern economic factors, for he had been born in a Durham coalfield. His father had died when he was only five years old, and soon afterwards he had begun to earn his living by doing a newspaper round in the mornings before going to school.

One midday at the end of July, an R.A.F. bomber passed over the camp, flying from the direction of Ubol and turning away into the clouds towards the north-west. When the working parties came in later they brought in a story of pamphlets having been dropped on the town. The camp was soon full of rumours. It was said, without truth, that the Allies had landed in Japan, Tokyo was taken and the Emperor had gone to Manchuria. The Japanese at the aerodrome became nervous of the possibility of airborne landings by British troops, so the newly-finished runways were scored across with ditches, dug two yards wide and two deep, to prevent aircraft from using them. Breastworks were made on the central runway, and all materials were withdrawn within them. Any prisoners who co-operated with airborne troops would be shot. The men grumbled still about their work, the food and the ragged state of their clothes, but they concluded by saying, 'It won't be for long now.' Some planned a 'holiday with the wife.'

On the morning of 16 August only a small working party was taken out of the camp after roll-call. At the aerodrome the men were told to clean all the tools and put them away, as there would be no more work. They returned to the camp by midday. In the truck that had carried some of them (using charcoal for fuel) a broad-shouldered sergeant stood leaning over the roof of the driver's cab. The Korean in charge of the party took a piece of charcoal and wrote across the bare skin of his back, 'The war has finished. England has won.' In the camp uncertainty gave way to conviction, but there was no demonstration of excitement.

On the 17th of August no working parties had been called for. The prisoners stood on parade at the usual time and were counted. The Japanese commandant, wearing his clumsy ceremonial sword, stood facing them. He told them, through the Dutch interpreter, that no more work would be required, because the war between the Japanese and the British was finished. He warned them, however, not to leave the camp, because large bands of Japanese soldiers were roaming the countryside in a mood of desperation and they would certainly kill any prisoners whom they might meet. The prisoners listened in silence and without movement, for they had learnt to be patient.

In the evening, the Thai governor of Ubol sent a lorry-load of food into the camp. He reiterated the Japanese commandant's warning against leaving the protection of our stockade. Within a few days a big Dakota was roaring over our heads, dropping bales of food and clothes and medical supplies from India. In a week or two we began to go short distances outside the camp. The rains ceased, but the poor, sandy soil remained saturated with water. With a Dutch friend I followed the tinkling bells of the buffaloes, pastured outside our stockade, to the village where they belonged, a group of huts built on stakes and platforms beneath a few palm-trees. Between the huts the peasant women were unwinding the threads of silk from the cocoons of silkworms. At the entry to the village four British soldiers, seated on the ground, were talking to some children who stood smiling nearby. A young mother sat watching, and suckling her baby.

Arrangements were made for the British prisoners-of-war to leave this remote place at the end of September. With a curious mingling of dignity and abasement the Japanese officers and the gunso, Takashima, came to the gate of the camp to salute us as we went. We were taken to Ubol in lorries, along the dusty road between the green paddy fields. Many of the friendly townspeople came to the riverside to see us go. As a result of the rains the river was in flood and now it flowed broad and strong, nearly two hundred yards in width. We crossed in sampans, the boatmen working all day to carry the twelve hundred men over. From the rail-head on the other side of the river the train carried us to Bangkok. The Dutch prisoners remained at Ubol.

At the airport Dakota troop-carriers were waiting on the ground, and others were on their way from Rangoon, for we were to be flown to Burma. The R.A.F. crews, friendly but serious, went steadily about their jobs of testing and refuelling the machines. We climbed in and sat close together on the floor. As the planes rose, one after another, the world beneath us became a tessellated floor of green rice-fields, which all at once lost their inhabitants; birds, men and buffaloes disappeared. We passed through clouds, peering through the gaps in their white, rounded masses at the river and the jungle, far below. For a moment we had a glimpse of the thin, curving line of the railway that we had built. We shivered, for at 13,000 feet the air was cold. We saw

66

clouds, jungle again, and a wide river-estuary; then a long strip of yellow sand, edged with breaking surf, which separated the sea from the jungle. The coast was left behind; beneath us was the green sea, the Gulf of Martaban, its surface wrinkled. Then another coast was seen, with another estuary, the river Irawaddy. The pattern of rice-fields was repeated, a human population was projected among them as I saw a man paddling a canoe. We circled over a great city, whose golden pagodas were shining points among the roofs of the streets. This was Rangoon, in Burma.

Rangoon had the stir and bustle of a city in military occupation; army-trucks and lorries jolted along the roads, and transit-camps fringed the outskirts. Three or four sea-going ships were berthed in the river. Rangoon had been shelled and bombed twice, first by the Japanese invasion and again three and a half years later. Broken roofs had never been repaired, and crumbled house-fronts allowed a view of trees growing inside the walls. (In the moist tropical climate their growth had been rapid.) But in spite of these vestiges of war the Burmese were walking freely and at ease through the streets, and food was on sale in the shops. The city became dark at dusk, but one evening I heard a sound of flutes and drums, and when I looked through the gateway into a courtyard I saw a wedding-procession moving along under the light of burning torches of resinous wood. The flames, held high overhead, lit up the gaily-coloured clothes and golden ornaments of dancers and revellers.

We were taken to a transit-camp to await embarkation. The camp was a collection of huts and tents spread over a hillside, about ten miles out of Rangoon. We had insufficient water for washing ourselves, so in the evenings we took buckets to the well beside a neglected Buddhist shrine and sluiced ourselves down with its earthy dregs, to remove the sweat. In this camp we were entertained one evening by the witty and warm-hearted singer, Gracie Fields. She stood on the level tail-board of a lorry, wearing a man's jungle-green uniform, and for a moment she seemed almost to be in tears as she faced the rows of released prisoners who sat on the bare ground in front of her. Then, stepping forward to the edge of her narrow platform, she asked, 'Oo's sweating?'

'All of us!' the men roared, delighted.

In Rangoon I went to the hospital where released Indian prisoners were under treatment, and made enquiries for Col. Dutta. I was told that he was still in Singapore, refusing to leave until the last of the sick men in his care had begun their journey for home. For three and a half years he had contrived to run a hospital for the Indian troops who were working in the docks and the harbour-area. He had saved many lives, I was told, with very little help from the Japanese, who had, in fact, made many difficulties.

We were taken from the transit-camp to the harbour in lorries and went aboard a troop-ship, which lay anchored in the river, a mile or two below the city. Looking back, we saw the buildings on the waterfront; they seemed quite small. On both sides of the river the country lay flat, green and featureless. Only behind the city the Schwe Dagon pagoda stood upright on its bushy knoll, with the afternoon sunshine reflected goldenly from its smooth and gracious curves.

Twenty-four hours earlier I had entered the courtyard surrounding this great and beautiful building. I walked slowly around it; then I rested my arms on a low wall or parapet, leaning forward to look over the house-tops to the river and the green rice-fields beyond. I became aware of a Burmese who stood beside me. 'Yes,' he said gently, 'it is very beautiful. I would guess,' he added, 'that you have been a prisoner-of-war with the Japanese.'

I looked at him and saw a man slightly older than myself, bare-headed and wearing a white shirt and khaki trousers. 'Yes,' I said; 'I have been a prisoner-of-war.'

'I also,' continued the Burmese. He spoke English without difficulty. After a pause he added, 'We have no reason to love the Japanese. They took everything they wanted from our country and from our people. Now we must build our lives again. You will be going home to England?'

'Yes,' I said.

'If you have any hate for the Japanese you must leave it behind you. You worked on the railway?'

'Yes.'

'I also,' said the other again. 'We worked in the forest on this side of the mountains. The Japanese were very cruel. Many of my companions died and are buried in the forest. You English know how it was.'

'Yes.'

'They killed many of my friends.' The man said it without hatred; and I understood that he had left his hatred behind him. I looked closely at his face and wondered what brutalities had so scarred and seamed it. This man, I thought, had learned the secret of endurance, and his brown eyes were peaceful.

The ship veered to the north. The wide waters of the Red Sea narrowed to the Bay of Suez. Here, on either hand, we saw the desolate hills of Arabia and Egypt. They were bare, yellow sandstone, seamed and excoriated; their flanks were streaked by gullies lying in shadow. On one side of the Bay were the tall houses of Suez; on the other, at Adabaya, a tented camp stretched along the seashore. We disembarked at Adabaya from lighters. The steel cranes were fluttering with coloured flags; the red hammer and sickle hung beside the more familiar emblems of Britain and the U.S.A. On the wall by the jetty, curls and loops of red bunting cried, 'Welcome from the Middle East Forces. Bon Voyage.' A train was waiting in the sunshine to take us to the depot two miles away. Again in the big open sheds the flags were suspended; we were fitted with new and warmer clothes. We were all touched, I think, by the kindness and friendliness of the camp staff; we might have been conquering heroes instead of the remnants of a beaten army. The camp itself was no more than a patch of tent-lines in the monotony of the desert. German prisoners, taken in Libya or Tunis, were lounging in the shade of the buildings. Our own men, two months free, threw cigarettes to them from the train as they passed.

A long day saw us pass through the Suez Canal, a narrow waterway flanked by sand-dunes and ornamented by a few stunted palm-trees; a string of camels was tethered, motionless. A heap of twisted and rusty scrap-iron, dragged up onto the side of the canal, represented a ship that had been bombed. Two captured Italian cruisers were peacefully at anchor in the Great Bitter Lake; the scene of the long preparation for Alamein was deserted.

As we came slowly up the Mersey into Liverpool, feeling for the first time the cold of the northern climate, the ships we met sounded their sirens in greeting; little flags waved to us in the wind. The city looked grimy and sombre, but the tall buildings and sloping roofs, with twists of smoke coming from the chimney-stacks, seemed reassuringly familiar. A band played at the dock-side; friends and relatives who had come to meet us cheered bravely. They were mainly women and children, wrapped in overcoats and scarves and squeezed behind a barrier. I watched them curiously; these were the people who had endured the long years of tedium, danger and anxiety at home. The men on the ship hung over the rail, making little reply to this welcome, apparently listless. 'If I open my mouth I shall probably cry,' one of them said to me. I was sad myself as I walked the length of the deck, recognising individuals whom I had known, in one camp or another, during our captivity. These men were soon to be lost to me, as completely as their comrades whom we had buried in the jungle; already, as they began to file down the gangway, clad in heavy greatcoats and shouldering their kitbags, their look was unfamiliar.

Part Two

Note

These are extracts from the memories of a small number of ex-PoWs, mainly from the Dereham area of Norfolk. They should be treated like an album of word-pictures. They are in no way a complete account of the captivity, and because the time-gap is considerable and memory can play strange tricks, there may be errors in names and dates.
Place-names have to some extent been standardised, but every book on this subject contains different spellings of the camp names, because they were heard rather than read.

Prisoners of War

The following memories have been collected by Sue Palmer from surviving POWs and their relatives. They are of course only a few of the many who were imprisoned at the fall of Singapore. Most came from Norfolk, and their memories may help to fill out the picture drawn by Harold Churchill.

In alphabetical order the contributors are:

William Daniel ('Reg') Anthony
Born: 18.11.1914; died 2005
4 Howlett Close, Dereham - 01362 695328

Able-Seaman C. Bishop, RN
Dereham
Gunner aboard the *Repulse*

Bertie Charles Boyce
Royal Norfolk Regiment
Born : Dereham
4A Dene Park, Harrogate, North Yorks. HG1 4JY. 01423 530216

Nelson D. Brighty
Private, 6th Battalion, Royal Norfolk Regiment
5, Mattishall Lane, Hockering

Ted Brown
Sergeant, Cambridgeshire Regiment
Source: His widow, Mrs Rae Brown, 65 Havenfield, Cambridge
01223 501230

R.J. (Reg) Bullard
Private 5774576 5th Battalion Royal Norfolk Regiment
Born 16.01.1917; died 1996
15 Paradise Road, Bawdeswell
Source: David M. Oldfield (son in law), 17 Hall Road, Bawdeswell,
Dereham NR20 4SQ. 01362 688572.

Harry Cassidy
Leading Aircraftsman, RAF
Born: 10.08.1918,
10 Gordon Road, Dereham 01362 694546

Eric Arthur Cullum
4th Battalion Royal Norfolk Regiment
5775119 13 Platoon C Company
Born: 20.06.1921 at Diss, Norfolk
6 Heidi Close, Toftwood, Dereham. 01362 696657

Eric Dack
5th Battalion Royal Norfolk Regiment
Born: Billingford 1919

Charles ('Charlie') Frost M.M.
Born 03.05.1921,
17 Orchard Close, North Elmham

William A. ('Bill') Garrod
5th Battalion Royal Norfolk Regiment
Born 07.04.1919,
33 Fakenham Road, Lenwade. 01603 872538

Sid Greenwood
Sergeant 4th Battalion Royal Norfolk Regiment
Source: His son, Raymond Greenwood, 17, Tebbitt Avenue, Dereham (born
1936 at Larner's Drift, Toftwood). 01362 695328.

Reginald James Griffin
Born 14.12.1918; died 10.11.2004
18 Albert Myhill Close, Dereham. 01362 853065

Fred Hoskins
Born: 1916; died February 2005
Hope Springs, Scarning

Derek (Dick) Langley
5th Battalion Royal Norfolk Regiment
Born 19.3.1919
65 Bradenham Road, Shipdham

Joseph (Joe) Walter Mason
Private 1st Battalion, Royal Norfolk Regiment
Stone Cottages, Westfield Road, Dereham
Born Bethnal Green 24.01.1908; died 25.03.1985
Source: Fred Mason (son), 2 Breton Close, Toftwood, Dereham.
01362 698729.

Richard (Dick) Osborne
18 Division, 4th Battalion, Royal Norfolk Regiment
Born Mattishall 24.06.1919
12 Back Lane Mattishall. 01362 850035

George Edward Parnell
Private 5774366 5th Battalion Royal Norfolk Regiment
Born: 03.05.1921; died: 28.06.1999
47 Sandy Lane Dereham Norfolk

Bertie Perkins
Private 5776768 5th Battalion Royal Norfolk Regiment
Born: 23.04. 1919; died 1993
38 Becclesgate, Dereham

Jim Quadling
Private, 5th Battalion Royal Norfolk Regiment
Born 30.8.1919
Of Toftwood and Yaxham

Reginald Herbert ('Busty') Rudd
Private 4th Norfolks
Born 23.02.1919 at Reepham,
86 Richmond Rise, Reepham

John Arthur Weales,
Born 15.06.1919,
6, Bayfield Avenue, Dereham, 01362 853312

John (Jack) Whitehead
Sherwood Foresters
Born Edmonton, London 22.02.1917
90 Doris Barnes Court, Dereham. 01362 851505

The following prisoners are also mentioned by name in the extracts below:

Sidney Bales, General Beckwith-Smith, Paul Borough, Reggie Brown, RSM L. Burrows, Bob Cocks, Padre Dean, Padre Duckworth, Captain Escritt, Captain Douglas Gray, Pte Giles, G. Hardiment, Corporal Hathaway, Sid Hooks, Reginald Hubbard, Captain Michael Keith, Captain Kerrison, Basil Leggett, Pte Lightwing, Lt Col. Pratley, Padre Ross, Sid Saunders, Barham Savory, Dr Taylor, Tom Vincent, Captain Wallace, Dr de Wardener, Lt Witherick.

Fred Hoskins wrote his own illustrated account of his captivity in 1992, entitled *The Fall of Singapore & the Thai-Burma Railway.* Several extracts and two drawings from this excellent account are included below with permission from his family.

Eric Dack, Nelson Brighty and Reggie Griffin also wrote their own accounts. Sincere thanks are due to those who have allowed extracts from their stories to be printed here.

**Dereham POWs twenty-five years after the end of the war,
at the George Hotel, Dereham**
Back row: H. Green, W. Craske, E. Skipper, Dr W. Dowell, Major R. Ferrier,
E. Brunton, H. Cassidy
Front Row: E. Dack, B. Perkins, J. Quadling, W. Garrod, S. Hagan

74

The Journey Out

At the end of October 1941 the 5th Battalion of the Royal Norfolks embarked from Gourock on the Duchess of Atholl. Among the 6,600 or so aboard were

Bill Garrod *of North Elmham*

'Being in the Territorial Army I automatically joined up at the beginning of WW2 ... Our training started in Dereham where the 14 lads were billeted in the Fleece in Norwich Street. ... The people who kept the Fleece were paid a guinea a man a week to feed us. From Dereham we went into private billets at Holt and later to Weybourne Camp. Whilst there, 60 plus men were picked to go to Sandringham to do guard duties for the royal family during their Christmas stay. On Saturday nights 30 men would be invited to the pictures in the ballroom with the royal family, guests and servants.

Here we did 24 hours guard, next day on a cadre course, next on fatigues. One fatigue I was on was to sweep the ice rink on the frozen lake between the intervals of ice-hockey games, for which we got awarded 10 cigarettes and a bottle of beer.

While we were at Sandringham the rest of the battalion went clearing the railway of snowdrifts. After five weeks we went back to Weybourne to find no water; all the pipes and tanks were frozen hard or split. Water for washing was snow melted down in a 5-gallon container on a tortoise stove.

In May 1940 we left the Camp and went into the hills around Weybourne, Kelling and Salthouse ... In the autumn we were billeted in Gresham's School, quite luxurious compared with the next in King's Lynn, where we slept 300 men on the fourth floor of a seven-storey grain store. Barley haulms had got into the floor cracks and we found them in all our kit. We felt rather hard-done-by but we didn't know what was coming.

We were on manoeuvres in Scotland from Jan–April 1941 – sometimes sleeping in farm buildings, sometimes in bivouacs. There was a long stay at Marbury Hall near Northwich, then we went to Gourock to board the *Duchess of Atholl*. We crossed the Atlantic to Halifax, Nova Scotia, and were transferred to the USS *Mount Vernon*, which took us to Port of Spain, Trinidad, then went south into the Antarctic to avoid U-boats and north again to Cape Town.

When I was in the Signals Office at Marbury Hall I got the word that we were going to Iraq. We set sail for Bombay, but never got there; instead, we landed in Singapore.

After two days the 5th and 6th Norfolks and the 2nd Battalion Cambridgeshires were loaded into transport trucks and headed for Malaya.'

Charlie Frost
I joined the Territorials when I was about 16. When war broke out I automatically joined the 5th Royal Norfolk Regiment and became an infantryman – 9th of Foot....

I finally sailed from Gourock with the 18th Division on the *Duchess of Atholl*, called 'The Drunken Duchess' because she was a ship fitted out with wood; pegs were loose everywhere and she wallowed in bad weather.

John Weales, Reg Bullard *and* **George Parnell** *(a cowman who had been at school in Guist – 'Guist High School' because you had to go up seven steps to get in!) were also aboard the Duchess, and so was*

Reggie Griffin. The voyage was uneventful until we reached Halifax which was approximately 8 am on Saturday November 8 and was nice to see all the lights on again; all the ships were lit up.

We then had to change over ships. This time we went on to an American ship called the USS *Mount Vernon*, 30,000 tons, which was formerly the liner *Washington...*

...There was about 6,000 of us on this boat and 600 crew; it was a bit crowded, three beds high; it was lovely sleeping on top deck on this boat as the weather got very hot. Food was fairly good till the army started in the ship's galley and they stopped us from having too much food....

We were then supposed to be going to Cairo Egypt; that was the general rumour. The weather up till now has been pretty good, but a lot warmer than it is at home. On Sunday 23 at 1 o'clock we crossed the equator. The ceremony of crossing the line was carried out and nearly everybody on board either had a cock-eyed hair cut or a good soaking from the hoses. On December 9 we reached Cape Town South Africa. During our stay we all had a very good time. The people were waiting to take us out on the spree and take us to their homes. We were all very sorry to leave. ...

On Thursday 18 December we were told that our destination was Bombay; five days later 23rd we turned back, not knowing where we were going, leaving the rest of the convoy behind. When we left them we were all alone, heading for Mombasa at 1.30 pm. On Xmas Day and Boxing Day we were allowed ashore; we had plenty of time to look around. It was very hot here; my pal and I went to a café and all the beer in there was half a crown a bottle...

On Monday 29 December we set sail at 10.30 pm and on Tuesday 30th met another convoy. Our destination is now supposed to be Singapore.'

Also sailing from Gourock, but in the Athlone Castle, was **Harry Cassidy.**

'I left Gourock, after training as a medical orderly, during the night of the 7 December 1941 on the *Athlone Castle*. We had no idea of our des-tination but had been issued with tropical kit (including pith helmets which turned to cardboard in rain and disintegrated).

We crossed the Atlantic and the Indian Ocean and first landed at Durban in South Africa. On the voyage, we noticed that some of them had K and others P on their kitbags. At Durban, all the Ks stayed behind and eventually went to the Middle East. All the Ps, including me, continued on through the Banka Straits towards Singapore. When we were nearly there, we were bombed in daylight by Japanese planes. Luckily we had changed ships and were now aboard the *City of Canterbury*, a smaller and much more manoeuvrable vessel, escorted by the *Ajax* and the *Ramillies*. Two naval men were killed in the attack, but their captain managed to steer a zigzag course and most of the men, including me, were unharmed.'

Others, **Dick Osborne, Busty Rudd** *and* **Eric Cullum,** *sailed from Liverpool on the Andes, transferring at Halifax, Nova Scotia, to the Wakefield.*

Dick Osborne *of Mattishall* 'embarked from Liverpool in 1941 on the *Andes*. It was like a cork popping about. We became part of the 18th Division, 4th Battalion, Royal Norfolk Regiment. Our first stop was at Halifax, Nova Scotia, where we transferred to the USS *Wakefield* – a luxury liner. We had been issued with tropical kit and thought we were destined for the Middle East.

The next stop was Cape Town where we were allowed ashore....We re-embarked on the same ship and were in the Indian Ocean on 9 December, when we heard about the bombing of Pearl Harbor. We continued to Bombay and unloaded and settled in a camp nearby at Ahmednagar for 2–3 weeks, then it was back to Bombay and onto the *Wakefield* again. We had been taking a zig-zag course across both Atlantic and Pacific oceans to avoid submarine attack.

On 27 January 1942 we reached Singapore.'

Busty Rudd, *a bricklayer from Reepham,* 'I was an 'M'. My friends marked' 'K' went to the Middle East. We all knew that Singapore was a fortress island that could resist any invasion, and we were not too worried about the Japs as we were told "they are all little people, who wear spectacles and are frightened of the dark."'

Eric Cullum, *who trained as a medical orderly, said that after sailing from Halifax in the Wakefield,* 'We went down the coast of America and called at Rio de Janeiro where the entertainment officer bought an old piano. He asked on the tannoy:

"Is there a piano tuner aboard?" and a man appeared, even carrying his key. You would be surprised what skills we had among us – tinsmiths, the Manager of London Brick, carpenters, bricklayers, all sorts of trades.'

Jack Whitehead *followed a similar route, but sailed in the Orcades and transferred to USS West Point at Halifax.*

'I left for Singapore in Oct 1941 from Liverpool in the *Orcades* and first landed at Halifax, Nova Scotia. The USS *West Point* took us to Cape Town. I was into music and did two shows in Cape Town. The Dagenham Girl Pipers were there at the time and we combined as a Concert Party. I played any keyboard instrument, in this case a piano-accordion. I met Dennis East, a violinist, who ended up as the Leader of the London Philharmonic Orchestra.'

Bertie Boyce *of Dereham* 'enlisted in the Territorial Army, Royal Norfolk Regiment in June 1939 when I was 17½ years old the minimum acceptance age.

At that time, I worked for Mr Kerrison, Church Street, the butcher's shop. I was an errand boy delivering orders and helping in the shop. Mr Kerrison was known by the name 'Totty', but as a lad I was careful he did not hear me.

On Friday 2 September 1939, I was called up for duty and ordered to report to the Drill Hall up Norwich Road. I told Mr Kerrison that I would not be able to come to work now as I was called up. He was very cross and said I would have to be at the shop first and get the weekend customers' orders delivered before I went to play soldiers. I told him that I could not. With that he went up to the Drill Hall and saw RSM Humphreys and told him he wanted me at the shop 'as it was a busy day on Saturdays.' Well, the RSM had a few strong words to say to 'Totty'. He never got me to the shop, so from then on my life changed and little did I know how it would change. At the time, I was very happy to be in the army, away from 'Totty' who at times was rather hard on me. He would give me a clout sometimes - well, perhaps I deserved it. I had the habit of taking my harmonica around and sometimes stopped somewhere to play so I would get back to the shop late. One day he found out and he gave me a few clouts. I took no notice of him and carried on as usual. It was how it was in those days. But he was rather upset about me getting called up. He was only thinking about me really, but it did not work out. I was now on active service.

...We left on October 4 1941 to Nova Scotia and had a rough crossing.

78

We then sailed down to the South Atlantic and to South Africa, Kenya, Ceylon (as it was known then) but by then Japan was at war and that changed things; we went full steam ahead to Singapore. We docked, just missing an air attack as Japanese bombers came after the convoy, but we were in luck because a sudden tropical storm arrived. The heavy dark clouds hid our ship so saved us from attack and we got to our destination safe and sound.'

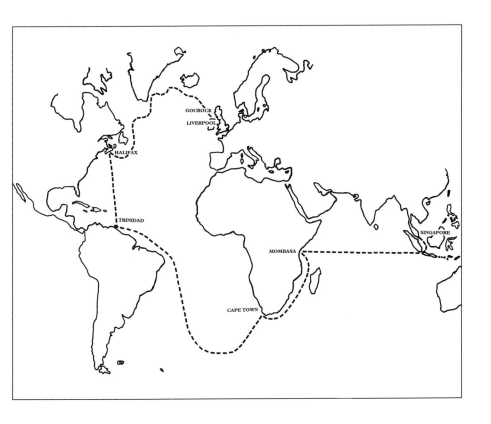

Sea route to Singapore

Surrender

When the troops landed at Keppel Harbour the situation on Singapore Island was confused, the Japanese having moved south much quicker than expected. In general the Chinese and Thai people were helpful to our troops, but many Malays were on the side of the Japanese.

Fred Hoskins. 'On landing on Singapore Island, we found ourselves in an unreal world. The island is connected to the mainland by a Causeway across which ran a railway line and the water supply for the whole of the island. Fleeing from invading Japanese forces were thousands of Tamils, Chinese, Thais and Malays, all looking alike to our western eyes and thus making it easy for Japanese fifth columnists to infiltrate. ...

In planning the defence of Singapore Island, it had been thought that any attack must come only from the sea on the south side of the island as there are mangrove swamps on the northern coast which were thought to be impenetrable. The heavy naval guns were therefore constructed to sweep out to sea on the south side of the island and not to the north. It was impossible to swing them completely around if attacked from the north. As we landed on Singapore Island crack Japanese troops assembled on the southern tip of Malaya in readiness for attack.'

Jack Whitehead. *While they were still at sea in the Indian Ocean,* 'General Percival, the 18th Battalion General, got through to the War Office to say "don't let them land," but was not listened to. We hadn't a chance from then on.

As we landed in Keppel Harbour, women and children were evacuating onto the same ship and some of the soldiers doubled back and stowed away. ... They were still in Singapore on 15 February 1942, the day of the capitulation.

I remember standing on the dockside outside Raffles Hotel looking for a boat to escape in, but all escape routes were already barred – Java, Sumatra etc. already taken over by the Japs. We were trapped.'

Dick Osborne. 'On 27 January 1942 we reached Singapore. Our job there was at the docks, to unload an army transport ship carrying trucks, Bren carriers, etc. At the same time, Singapore civilians were evacuating themselves on the same ship, the *Empire Star*. We were told we could take what we liked from the dock warehouses; there was tinned stuff and all sorts. Many men got very drunk as they took whole cases of whiskey.

One morning, in particular, we saw a convoy of ships 10 miles out. They

80

bombed the *Empress of Asia*; people were coming ashore any way they could, in little boats, sampans, rowing boats, anything. We were being bombed in Singapore harbour as we were unloading. There was a mass of black smoke. The Jap planes came over 27 at a time and dropped their bombs from some height. ...

I remember 15 February 1942. ... British officers came to tell us we had to lay down our arms. We were under orders so we had to do as we were told.'

Busty Rudd. 'We landed in Singapore some time in January 1942 and were immediately in action near the Johore Causeway. This had already been blown up to prevent a Japanese landing from the north, but part of the structure was still there and the Japs made short work of restoring it with logs and were soon able to drive their tanks across in the darkness.

They fired mortars at us, always in the same formation, one at each corner of an imaginary square, then a concentration in the middle. We got used to spotting where the first mortars landed and then got out of the centre of the square. One man went berserk, shrieking and jumping about. We had to hold him down. Not many of our men were killed – only three in Singapore.'

Charlie Frost. 'After nearly three months at sea we reached Keppel Harbour in Singapore and first went into a holding camp. After two or three days there, we were enjoying a boozy evening in the NAAFI when the order came "Get your kit. We're off." We were feeling none too fit as we climbed into the lorries in the dark and drove over the one mile causeway to Malaya.

Near Kuala Lumpur we came upon a road block. Trees had been felled across the road. Machine guns and Japanese soldiers were everywhere. Our unit had to abandon our vehicles and begin fighting on foot. I was in charge of a machine gun as we came to a cross roads. We split into sections and I and my mate Private Lightwing (who was killed later) lay on either side of our gun, frightened in the dark. We agreed to whistle three times if we heard anything. There was no need to whistle as we heard a lot of marching and chattering coming towards us. We let seventeen magazines into them till the barrel was red hot. It was a landing party of Japs. Then a bren gun carrier came with Barham Savory, who took control.

We ran back to the cross roads and I hid under a concrete bridge spanning a stream. Japs were firing mortars and my tin hat was hit; it was dented, but there was no real damage. We were picked up in a lorry and I and Sid Hooks *[of Fakenham]* had a bren. Sid was badly injured in his shoulder and had to be taken to Kuala Lumpur.

As I returned towards Singapore, I met up with other soldiers, but when we reached the bridge over the water, it had been blown up. I was put onto the front of an ambulance as a guard but in the end we had to give up. We had to leave our vehicle and take to the jungle on foot. Some were walking wounded. It was all very frightening. We were 5 days in the jungle. Once I fell into a muddy dyke and couldn't get out; other men were clambering over me.

Eventually we reached the west coast of Malaya and waited in a mangrove swamp; when the tide came in we were in water up to our necks. We were picked up in small boats, which took us to Singapore. We had had nothing to eat for 5 days and were picked up in trucks and found a warehouse where we helped ourselves to lots of foodstuffs. When we reached the camp, we were medically checked, given a new clothing issue and boots. Our old boots had had to be cut off after our time in the swamps. We heard later that we could have swum across from Malaya to Singapore – it was only a mile – but there were alligators!

After a day or two we were sent out to fight again. We were in naval docks and Japs had crossed the mangrove swamps and come inland. We were saved by some Gurkhas – one gave me a string of ears, all dripping blood, and said, "You can keep those Johnnie". ...

We found ourselves near a reservoir on a road where Jap soldiers were driving local women and children ahead of them as a human shield against attack. We had to fire over them. There was an outpost on a big hill near a cemetery where we spent the night. One of the guards was found next day with his head criss-crossed with slashes and his nose cut off. He had been left for dead by his Jap attackers. We loaded him onto a stretcher and took him to hospital and they put him right. He was lucky to survive.

The next night it was my group's turn to do sentry duty on the hill. They included a very green 1st Lieutenant from Attleborough who was always asking what he ought to do, and a corporal. [*Charles seems to have been the leader. He had been a Lance Corporal in England, but lost his stripe through taking 'agricultural leave'.*] The guards lay in a circle, all within arm's reach of each other so they could wake each other up if there was an incident. ... The Japs surrounded us with mortars. The guards tried to get out but couldn't. After two or three days they made an attempt again, but a mortar blew up. My brother had a lump out of his leg and another man had his brains blown out. One lad came to help us but received a single bullet in the neck. No it didn't kill him. He later became a jockey at Newmarket.

We then heard General Percival had surrendered - we would certainly have gone on fighting. We had to pile up our rifles and the Japs came and collected them and took us prisoner. If you had a watch or any valuables with you they asked for them. They asked for our rings and if we couldn't get them off our fingers, they took them, finger and all.'

Charles Frost received the Military Medal for his part in the action described above.

82

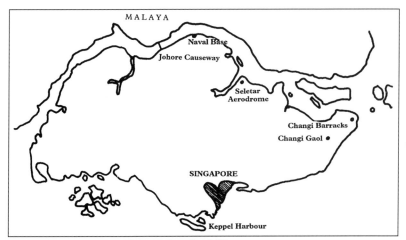

The Island of Singapore

Bill Garrod. 'When we got to Singapore, we landed in a storm of rain and got drenched. We settled in the Naval Base and remained a couple of days to dry out. We were told to leave our kit there and never saw it again. We were sent to Malaya with just a haversack, rifle, small pack and gas cape and went up the east coast about 120 miles to take over from the Aussies.

Japs were coming down east and west coasts and turned inland. The 6th Norfolks got surrounded and cut off; the 5th Norfolks were working there to assist. In the meantime the 6th Norfolk's reinforcement company of 120 men was on its way, but was ambushed and machine-gunned before the men could get off the trucks. Only 14 men survived. They had been left for dead in a ditch. Sid Saunders, a man from Attleborough way, heard moaning and found them. I met up with him in Changi. He later died on the Railway. Also killed in the ambush was Sergeant Reginald Hubbard from Worthing near North Elmham. He was a Sergeant Signaller in the 6th Norfolks. The 5th Norfolks *[including Bill Garrod and Charles Frost]* who had gone to help the 6th, found themselves surrounded. There was a roadblock. Some wounded got through in an ambulance, but one was found with a revolver, so passage for the rest was stopped.

The ambulances were sent back into a local town Nong Peng where the wounded were put into shops. Those who couldn't walk were shot. Padre Duckworth volunteered to stay with the sick. ...

Eventually we had to go back over the river – the bridge had been blown up and we were being fired on. We had to wade and swim. We were told to take off our shirts and put our bandoliers next to our skin and loosen all other equipment so that it could be abandoned and wouldn't drag you down and drown you.

83

Michael Keith (from Hoe Hall near Dereham) was our adjutant. He was 6ft 6 inches tall so could plough a way through a jungle. He kept swigging from a flask. We heard bushes snapping and waited to see if it was friend or foe. It was a party of Sikhs.

We all stopped to have a rest with our group in the middle and the Sikhs in a ring, head to toe, round the outside. We managed to sleep with their protection, but next morning the Sikhs had all come in close. There was no water, so I found a coconut, but we had no bayonet to open it, so I carried it along. When we stopped next time we were in a coconut plantation!

We shot our way out of Malaya and over the Johore Causeway back to Singapore Naval Base. There we were taken prisoner and sent to Changi village.'

Reggie Griffin. 'Went to a camp and settled down for the night with only half a mug of tea and nothing to eat, which we all thought was a bad show on the army side. The huts were very good; we all thought that this was too good a place for us as we had a good bed, two sheets and a mosquito net. Next morning we had half a round of bread and half a slice of bacon and a mug of tea. After breakfast an officer, who was supposed to have been in action, gave us a lecture on what to do and what not to do. When we got in contact with the Japs all this turned out to be a lot of eyewash. They then told us we were moving up into Malaya to action.

Saturday January 17 we were taken by trucks up country. After a day or two of messing about in the good old army fashion we found ourselves at a place called Ayer Hitam. It was there that we had our first dose of action and lost some of the boys. It certainly shook us up a bit I'm afraid. A few days of that and we moved to the west coast to Batu Pahat where we again had another cut at the Japs. The night we arrived we spent on the roadside till about 2.30 in the morning, then we moved up to take up positions in a wood. When dawn broke, instead of the Japs being in front of us, they had encircled us and we were fired on from the rear and both flanks. We had then to withdraw, all those who could do so. That was after we had the order, "every man for himself", so we done the best we could and made our way through the jungle drinking coconut milk and any water we could get .... When we got through we met up with the rest of the boys again who did not go up country with us; that was nearly in Singapore again. They had a good meal ready for us and a good mug of tea with plenty of rum in it which made us sleep that night as we had no sleep the night before....

We had three days rest in Singapore and were allowed out in the town. Then we had to go back to make a front line for Singapore up against the Naval Docks. We dug ourselves in positions, stopped there a week then had to withdraw again because the Japs had landed and were getting round the back

84

of us again. Dug some more positions that morning and in the afternoon had to leave them. On the move this time we got bombed; several got killed. Tom Vincent got badly cut about and died later on. Gone back a good way into Singapore where we made our last stand. Till the day of Sunday when we had to fly the white flag, Feb. 15th 1942.'

Eric Dack. *At Ayer Hitam.* 'We soon found out that the Japs had landed further down the coast, and it was in this area I saw for the first time some of my dead comrades. I came across them and when I told my officer what I had found, he asked if I had looked at the identity discs, and because I had not I had to take him back to the spot where I had found them; there were four altogether.'

Dick Langley. 'We reached Singapore in late January 1942 and were fairly soon sent into battle in Malaya. I remember Batu Pahat, but I think I went further north than Kuala Lumpur. My unit was under the command of Captain Douglas Gray, the son of a Dereham coal merchant.

After fighting in Malaya my pals and I split up. Some went with Captain Gray in small boats to Colombo in Ceylon *[Sri Lanka]* and from there to India. Captain Gray died there. My best friend Bob Cocks *[the Dereham Postmaster]* went with him and carried on to fight in India, then Burma. He eventually returned home. I was with Eric Dack in the party that stayed in Malaya and we were involved in a nerve-racking rearguard action near a bridge which had been taken over by the Japanese. By this time we were being led by Captain Keith *[of Hoe Hall]*. He said, "We'll have to split up here. Some of us will get through and some won't."

Out of the blue came an officer of the Singapore Volunteers, who knew the area well. He was Captain Wallace. He led 20 or 30 of us from the Jap-held bridge and marched into the jungle straight south. I took only a rifle and dumped a now useless radio from my back. It was used for signalling and had heavy batteries. We were in the jungle for two or three days, guided by this local officer. He was marvellous. We had no trouble at all and kept to jungle paths. There was no food or water, but we found a few bananas.

Five miles further on we came to a camp which I think was manned by men from the RASC. Food was all cooked and ready. The Johore Causeway had not then been destroyed so we were able to march over it. We rested for a day or two as a reserve battalion just before the surrender.

On 15th February 1942 we were told to lay down our arms. We went into a clearing and piled up our rifles. Then we were marched to Changi Gaol.'

Eric Dack *was also led through the jungle by Captain Wallace.*
'Soon after this we had a very swampy area to pass through and it was not

long before we started sinking, some worse than others. I got stuck halfway up to my waist and was gradually sinking further. Two Indians in the same party quickly came to my aid and I held on to the butt of the rifle while they both got a grip on the barrel, and after a while they pulled me free. It was not long after this we disturbed a hornets' nest and they descended on us; some got away with only one or two stings, others more. I must have had about twenty on my neck and face and I felt terrible, all my strength seemed to go. I carried a small bottle of TCP and I put this on the stings. I felt weak and told my mates to leave me and press on, but they refused, and took it in turns to half drag and carry me until I felt better.'

Reg Bullard. 'On disembarking, the personnel of the 53 Brigade were transported to the golf course. On 17 January we were ordered up the east coast of Malaya to a place called Ayer Hitam and onwards to Yong Pen where some fierce action had taken place. We then made our way back down again and then up the west coast to Benut; here we rested in a school. A party had to go further ahead to Rengit Water Tower, where fierce fighting took place and to our great dismay we learned of the loss of two officers, Captain Kerrison, Intelligence, and Lt Witherick, the Defence Platoon Officer; two other ranks were killed, five died shortly afterwards and six missing.

We headed back to Singapore and took up a position near Seletar Drome. There weren't any of our aircraft, only five Hurricanes shot down. I would state that the Royal Artillery boys gave them hell of a pasting.

As at 4 pm on the 15 February, the order came to capitulate to save the lives of the civilian population on the island. From then on we had to carry what we could and march 15 miles to Roberts Barracks at Changi, which was to be our home for some time. Shortly afterwards … there were deaths from among the injured. The 5th Royal Norfolk Regiment Padre was one of the first to be buried in the cemetery within the compound. If I am correct, I think his name was Padre Dean.'

Bertie Boyce. 'After a few days, the Battalion was ordered up country into Malaya but by now the Japanese army had advanced rapidly down, closing in on their objective, Singapore. We were expected to hold them but all was lost.

I was sent down to Singapore with a few others and we went across the Bay to a small island offshore from Singapore City. There was a big arsenal of ammunition, shells etc. We were to guard it and keep watch on the local labour force employed to load the shells on the barges. These were mostly anti-aircraft shells as there was a great demand for them. The gunners were shelling bombers all the time. Many of the local force cleared off; some were getting caught in the raids and it was a problem trying to keep them. We were ordered not to let them leave the island but there was no way we could stop them. There was nothing we could do and lost a lot of men. We were returned to the mainland and told to report to our units, as there was a problem. We bribed a lorry driver to take us up the east coast and it was a very rough ride with the raids and rubble all over the place. We found our Battalion at a barracks over the Johore Causeway.

I was very weary and hungry having not eaten for a long time. But there was no time for that. I fell in line and then rather wearily marched to an abandoned Naval Base place facing Johore. We found food in the houses so we could at least feed ourselves. We had a ration truck come up daily but it got too risky for the driver who gave it up as mortar bombs were getting too close to him. Now almost all the units were back on Singapore Island and so the attack by the Japanese was about to begin and this was the prize they were after, but it would soon be over for us. We withdrew from the naval base to set up near Singapore City but all the time we were under fire and air attacks. A few of us, including me, were detailed to remain to try and hold back any advance so the Battalion could withdraw. At least most of the Battalion did get away but there were continuous air attacks; one plane came in low and strafed those of us at the back. We were trying to hold off any enemy advance but it was hopeless and this plane came in at us with guns firing and dropping some small bombs. My section was badly hit. All round were dead and wounded. I was the only survivor from my section and I was hit in both arms and very shaken.

I was picked up by the medics and had dressings put on my wounds and when a Chinese truck went past the medics ordered the driver to take me with some others to the 197 Field Medical RAMC. But, by the time we arrived there, I was the only one still alive.

I was given medical care and then sent down to Singapore City. The RAMC ambulance was full of wounded from some other attack. I sat beside the driver but it was a dodgy ride as there were all the time raids. We arrived in Singapore and the raids were now continuous. I was taken to Singapore General Hospital, which was already full with civilian wounded; it really was a dreadful situation. I was left for several hours waiting for the medics to deal with me. I was now very weak with losing so much blood. I did get help and into a ward very late at night.

Singapore was now under siege. The Japanese were closing in, surrounding the City. They captured the water supplies, which made it impossible to carry on for they had cut off what was needed most. There was no food to feed the hospital.

I had lost my clothes and had nothing at all, but a Chinese nurse came to my help when she found a pair of hospital trousers and wooden sandals. This was February 12th and three days later it was all over. I remember getting out of bed and managed to get a little water from a toilet cistern and the Chinese nurse found me a few biscuits and a small tin of sardines. After that, there was nothing.

There had been a massacre at Alexandra Hospital when the Japanese stormed in, killing nurses, doctors and some wounded as they lay in bed. They went to the Operating Theatre, killed the man on the table undergoing an operation, the doctor and the nurses. A few Japanese also came into the General Hospital and into where I was. A Jap officer came, looked at me and he was holding his sword as if he was about to use it, but he moved off. It was a tense moment and left me feeling very shaken.

Then we heard the news that Singapore had surrendered, but what was to be our fate? There had been mass evacuations. Many got away but, even so, some were captured. As they sailed off, several boats were bombed and sank; many women and children lost heir lives like that. In the hospital where I was, a few Salvation Army Officers volunteered to stay behind and help with the wounded, both civilian and military.

February 15 and it was all over.'

John Weales. 'We made camp outside the docks, where there was an ack-ack gun. There were oil terminal tanks there. Jap planes came over and bombed us and as they did so I dived for cover. I was in the cookhouse at the time, carrying a big bowl of fat and it spilled all over me.

We were told the Japs were afraid to attack in the dark; but when we were on guard at night and rubbed mosquito oil on our legs the Japs crept up on us as they could smell the oil.

We were in a submarine station near the docks and the warehouses were all open. We took boxes of tinned milk and fruit, but could find no booze. We were always short of water and used to go round all the rainwater tanks to get some.

We were in Singapore for a couple of weeks before surrender. I was putting up 'concertina wire' defences. As I did so a mortar came down beside me and I caught my left middle finger on a spike and slashed it badly. It was my trigger finger – I'm left handed, but right-eyed, so I always unsighted myself. After the injury I couldn't use a rifle, so that's why I went into the cookhouse.

We camped on Seletar aerodrome, where there was not much in the way of aircraft, mostly just dummies that the Japs were bombing. We ate with the RAF men. I was in the cookhouse looking after the reserve troops. Some had already gone to Malaya. We heard there had been a surrender when all the boys started coming back.'

Harry Cassidy. 'When we reached port, the *Empire Star* had docked ahead of us. We met some officers who told us we could go ashore and into the warehouses and help ourselves to anything we wanted. No alcohol was seen but plenty of cigarettes, chocolate etc. At the port, women and children were being loaded for evacuation.

Our boat left for Java and we ended up at Batavia *[now Jakarta]*, then on to the Dutch camp of Buizenborgh. After three weeks there, we went to Bandoeng. The Japs had declared this place to be an 'open town' and there I was taken prisoner and returned to Cycle Camp at Batavia.'

Fred Hoskins. 'A perimeter defence had been formed of Australian, Ghurka, Indian and British troops across the island, containing the docks. The Japanese were holding the north and west and were thrusting forward. Eventually the defence was penetrated on the west side and the line had to fall back to avoid being cut off. The ground held by the Allied troops was thus shrinking rapidly and within were thousands of refugees of all kinds ... The air-raids were now very frequent with no real opposition and there was little water supply other than drips from the taps.

In a dockside warehouse, we found a whole gammon and an Australian hat which I put on. As we hadn't eaten for some time and possessed a petrol stove, Private H put the gammon in a Dixie and somehow got enough water to start boiling it. The Australian hat proved invaluable later in the tropical sun, working on the railway in Thailand ... We also found an abandoned MG sports car. Corporal WS twisted together the wires of the starter and got the engine going.

A Japanese spotter plane came over and a nearby ack-ack post opened fire without success and we saw the plane turn out to sea and disappear. Perhaps half an hour later we saw Japanese aircraft approaching – the usual twenty-seven – I ran for a slit trench, but some Indians got there first, so I threw myself flat on the ground by a wall as the whole harbour erupted in flames and smoke. I heard something solid hit the ground between my legs. The ground seemed to leap in the air and then there was silence broken only by the crackle of burning debris ... Private H. was sitting on the ground with blood running from both wrists, the gammon and petrol stove had both vanished and I was astonished to see Private W. calmly taking photographs of the blazing warehouses and Chinese junks. He buried his camera in a tin at the foot of a coconut palm, hoping to retrieve it later. Together we made our way from the inferno to the Cable & Wireless building where we met up again with our Captain.

A quick roll call was taken and it was found that Sergeant D. was missing. Corporal WS. and I got into the MG sports car and drove back into the docks

89

with flames licking the tyres which I expected to burst. Rows of cars and lorries were now smouldering wrecks. Boats in the harbour were burning or sunk. An ammunition lorry was exploding nearby. In the slit trench, which I had nearly reached, lay dead Indians, killed by a direct hit. Of Sergeant D. we found nothing, so we returned to the others, only to find him with them. We had missed him in the smoke. The date was 15th February 1942.

There seemed to be complete chaos. The overhead cables of tramcars were down, as were many buildings. A tram lay on its side. We sheltered behind sandbags in the Cable & Wireless offices, hot, dirty and apprehensive. Night fell and the mosquitoes came out for their evening meal. Everywhere men talked in whispers, waiting, wondering and fearful. Then came a rumour. We had capitulated! No! Don't believe it! Keep your weapons, it's a trick!'

Captivity: Early Days – the Selarang Incident

The prisoners were contained in many different camps and barracks: Roberts Barracks, Farrar Camp, billets in Singapore City and Changi Barracks are all mentioned.

Bertie Boyce. 'The Japanese turned everyone out of the hospital. I was taken to some place and put in a building and left there with a few others. There was a radio there and we tuned in and we heard London Big Ben strike 12. The wireless was taken away and from then on we would never hear anything from home.

We were turned out after several days and had to make our way to the north east. This was a fairly long walk and it was a sight never to be forgotten. Men struggling along and all had got injuries. I was lucky for after a while a truck went by and I got a lift to up to Changi point. I was very pleased to find most of the Battalion were there, for I thought that they had got away, leaving me in the hands of the enemy. It was wonderful to see the Dereham men who were also pleased to see me, as they were not sure if I had survived.

What was going to happen now? Well, we set ourselves into a camp and made some sort of programme of order. I had not had any treatment for my wounds since my operation. My right arm was stinking and a mess, for the plaster on it was soaked in blood. It was a few more days before there was some sort of medical place set up and I got treatment. As the plaster was removed it was nasty with maggots all over it but it was cleaned up. I was in the makeshift hospital for a few weeks but there never was any medical supplies given. It was make do and mend. Bandages were washed and reused.

From now on life would not be the same. We were in the hands of an enemy who had no regard for the Geneva Convention and had no mercy for us who had surrendered. We had surrendered and therefore our lives were worthless. We had forfeited our lives and disgraced ourselves. This was how they saw us and we were made to bow and scrape to them all.

We were then used as a labour force for there was much cleaning up to be done. To set an example, should we try to escape (and some tried), they were quickly dealt with and beheaded in front of our Commanding Officer who was forced to witness it. It became clear to us we were now with a ruthless enemy who would do anything. We were cut off from the outside world without any news from home and we were just lost. The Japanese told us we would never go home. I remember that well for it became very real to us as the years passed.'

Busty Rudd. 'We were billeted in Singapore town and when the Japs came they drove us into shops and penned us there. If you were wounded and couldn't stand, they shot you.'

Charlie Frost. 'We were marched back to Changi Barracks and put into unfurnished rooms with concrete floors. We were issued with a groundsheet and a gas cape, but no clothes. All we had was what we were wearing – a pair of shorts and a singlet, soaked in blood, and our boots. We were given no blankets.

We were in Changi for several months, mostly pushing concrete blocks on huge heavy trolleys. If anything went wrong you were beaten up. The guards used whatever came to hand, a bamboo pole or an iron bar and hit any part within reach. If you could stay on your feet, you were OK. If you went down, they kicked you unmercifully.'

Jack Whitehead. 'We camped on Singapore Racecourse for about a week. We were mostly clearing bomb rubble in the docks. By that time all the warehouses were out-of-bounds and no food stocks were available to us. We were moved to a prison area in Roberts Barracks in Singapore and were there for about six months.'

Dick Langley. 'We were sent to work on the docks, pushing 40-gallon oil drums, which we did our best to sabotage by loosening the bungs.'

Dick Osborne. 'Next day *[February 16]* the Japs rounded us up and we went to River Valley. We were there clearing up for a week or so then they took us to Changi Barracks and from there to tents on the playing field.

*[In September 1942]*They wanted us to sign a paper saying we wouldn't try to escape. Everybody said "No". We were all taken to Selarang where

thousands of us were crowded into a space no bigger than Morrison's car park. There was no room to move. You had to sit on your kit. We were given rice and water. Then dysentery and malaria started, though I kept OK. We were there for about a week. In the finish it got so bad we had to give in. Four men tried to escape and were shot dead.

In the end our officers ordered us to sign and I vaguely remember being told we would not be held responsible for signing and that King George VI would forgive us. Then we all went back to Changi playing fields and got on with our jobs.'

Selarang, September 1942

Bill Garrod. 'We marched 14 miles to Changi Barracks and stayed there about two weeks, then went back to Singapore to what had been an evacuation camp for civilians. It was our job to clean and tidy it up. It had been on fire and there were some dead bodies and debris everywhere. After three weeks we went back to Changi for another two weeks. Then we were transported by lorry to River Valley camp. There were 2,000 building workers and Royal Engineers there. While I was at River Valley Camp, the bulk of the 5th Norfolks were sent to work in the docks in Singapore.

When 17,000 were asked to sign a "no escape" paper they refused. Then the Japs said they would kill all 17,000 plus 2,000 sick and wounded. Their officer General Beckwith-Smith told them they should sign "under duress" and that this would cover them after the war. High-ranking officers were sent to Formosa (now Taiwan). Beckwith-Smith died there.' *[Another source says he died of diphtheria on the voyage to Japan.]*

92

Reg Bullard. 'We had a party of the boys to go to Singapore on various work. Our Battalion C.O. Lt. Col. Pratley went with us and we were based at Farrar Park in tents. I am sure the boys enjoyed this break and one good reason was it gave us the chance to retrieve all that was any good, mainly tinned food or anything that could be sold to the Chinese. Bags of flour, dried fruit and marmite helped out rations. We had a Sergeant Suki in charge of the camp and he allowed his guards to let us pass back into the camp without a search.

We then moved on to Serongon Road here we had to repair and build the huts. I was working with RSM L. Burrows and got on very well with him. We did other jobs before we went back to Changi.'

Fred Hoskins. 'We were told to stack our arms. At that time I had a .38 Smith & Wesson revolver and a First World War Ross rifle but had used neither. I put my ammunition down a drain and discussed with Corporal WS. what we should do with the MG sports car. Push it over the harbour wall? Finally we decided to batter the engine with a hammer. As we did so, two Chinese came along and asked if they could have it. We agreed and they pushed it away. We had also acquired an Austin Seven and this we did push over the harbour wall.

It was then that the first triumphant Japanese soldiers started to appear, standing on the rear bumpers of cars as they drove past. We were careful to keep out of sight.

An order came from the Japanese that our unit was to go back through their lines to check the stock of food in a food depot. We ... climbed aboard our temperamental lorry and, with a Japanese guard who carried a rifle and bayonet, made our way past hoards of victorious Japanese. Customarily they wore rubber shoes which separated the big toe from the others ... invaluable in jungle warfare as they could climb trees easily. Many of them were now sitting at the side of the road, putting on Australian brown boots which they had looted....

We eventually arrived at a depot where we were put in a large garage behind vertical wooden rails so that we were in effect in a cage. Japanese soldiers came to look at us and then, becoming bolder, started taking our watches and rings. I hid my wedding ring down my sock. Nearby was a brewery where Tiger beer was brewed and the Japanese were getting steadily more drunk as the day wore on. Drunken Japanese came into the cage offering bottles of beer and then poured them over the men ... There was no drinking water or food, but somehow I acquired a bottle of beer.

As dark fell, we were hustled into a single-decker 'bus and driven off, again with a Japanese guard. I thought we were being taken away to be shot.

93

My ring was still in my sock and I still had the bottle of beer.

We arrived at a large concrete building which proved to be Selarang Barracks and were roughly searched, our few possessions being thrown on to the ground. The bottle of beer I placed on the ground a few feet away. I was searched, and then I retrieved it. I collected together my worldly possessions, some handkerchiefs, a blanket, a bottle of Bovril, a piece of candle and my mess tin with knife and fork. I also had the clothes I was wearing and my Australian bush hat.

We were ordered to the top floor of the building and an iron gate shut on us with an armed guard posted just outside. There must have been three or four hundred of us. ... At the far end were the latrines. There was no water in the taps and the toilets were blocked and overspilling. At rare intervals, the guard allowed a bucket of water to be collected from outside and much would be spilled as everyone crowded around. I got a little in my mess tin and added the Bovril. The bottle of beer was soon gone; we stayed there for three days.

On the ground floor were Japanese troops. On the first floor were Free Indians (who had transferred their allegiance to the Japanese). The word circulated that the Japanese had told the Indians that we had let them down and urged them to throw a hand grenade among us. There was nothing we could do except lie on the floor and keep quiet.

During the three days, a sack of flour was given to us and some kind of dough made. I had three slices during that time. On the morning of the third day we were ... told we were to walk to Changi by the coast road. ... We set out in a long straggling column, four soldiers abreast, and the escorting guards arranged themselves on either side. The pattern was to walk for fifty minutes, then rest for ten minutes then to continue in this fashion for two days. As we had not eaten properly for three days, this seemed a superhuman task.

Our route took us through kampongs (native villages) and from every window hung improvised Japanese flags, usually a white sheet with a red blob in the middle. We didn't blame the natives who watched in silence. They couldn't believe that the invincible British army had been defeated. Occasionally a small loaf would be thrown into the column and hurriedly concealed from the eyes of the guard.

We spent the first night, weary, with blistering feet, in some bungalows where there had obviously been some severe fighting. Wall mirrors were smashed and the floors littered with smashed furniture. ... Some sort of meal from cans was provided, but there was only the occasional drips of water from the taps. We had covered about half our journey.

The following day we formed the same straggling line, but many were in poor condition ... Even the armed guards now seemed indifferent as they too plodded along. ... We came to a hill and Sergeant D. who suffered from

94

asthma and was red in the face said to me "Staffy, if we stop before we go up this hill, I'll be all right, but if we don't, I'll have to fall out." I was glad of an excuse. "If you do, then I shall too." We continued up the hill and Sergeant D. stepped out of the line and into the coconut groves at the side of the road. I did likewise and our disappearance went unnoticed by the guards who plodded on with their heads down.

The column wound on and eventually disappeared out of sight. ... The day passed slowly and late in the afternoon we saw an amazing sight – a lorry crammed with Australian soldiers, some clinging on the outside, came along. We flagged it down and they said they were on their way to Changi and agreed to give us a lift. We clung perilously to the sides and eventually turned in to the camp.

Others of our unit were already there to greet us and while we lay exhausted on the floor of a hut Sergeant S. brought us each a biscuit with jam on it – luxury indeed.'

After the incident at Selarang there were few attempts at escape. There simply was no route out, and up-country in Thailand the natives were offered substantial rewards for giving up any escapees. Fred Hoskins records one attempt.

Fred Hoskins. 'A personal friend, Sergeant Y. had been ill with dysentery and malaria and he determined to escape. He, with another man, suddenly disappeared. They got as far as the river, where they were handed over to the Japanese by local Thais. They had taken with them some hardboiled duck eggs for food and a shirt sleeve filled with stones as a weapon. They did not stand a chance as there was nowhere they could go. It was impossible to live in the jungle and they dared not drink any water. Sergeant Y. was tied to a stake driven into the ground and we had to pass him on our way to work. He was kept there a few days in the tropical sun and then taken away.

After the war I received a letter from him. He had been taken to Singapore and kept in solitary confinement. One day he threw himself over a bridge intending to kill himself. Remarkably, he was not greatly hurt but was taken to Roberts Hospital for treatment. A guard checked on him each day but got more and more casual and he stayed there until the end of the war!'

One who did escape captivity was **Able-Seaman C. Bishop,** *a survivor from the Repulse, a destroyer sunk 100 miles out from Singapore. He and eight other sailors were picked up by another destroyer and taken to Java. There they spotted a small coaster with a cargo of 'now dead and very smelly chickens'. They managed to sail this vessel out to sea and after five days and nights they landed at Geraldton in Western Australia. They sailed on to Fremantle and were recruited into the Australian Navy.*

Food

According to one prisoner, food quickly became a major pre-occupation and almost the sole topic of conversation. Prison diet consisted mainly of rice, rice and more rice. With some ingenuity, extras could be obtained, and Red Cross parcels, rare and long-awaited, provided occasional bonanzas.

Reggie Griffin. 'When we first came to Singapore we worked for nothing, but now we get 50 cents every ten days. We have got a good Camp Commandant now and he let us go out and get a piano into camp to have a sing song. Three men and an officer are allowed to go out of the camp with a Jap and buy bananas, peanuts and pineapples. The things we used to pinch on working parties we gave to them to take and sell to the Chinese, not so as the Japs saw them. All we used to get was plain rice for dinner; sometimes the Japs would give us something to go with it. We had little loaves of bread come into the camp in the evening, 10 cents a loaf from the Chinese.'

Fred Hoskins. 'The food supplies were poor and were basically rice, to which was added such scanty supplies of tinned food as still existed. On one occasion the rice was full of lime and when cooked looked either yellow or purple. The eating of it was disastrous, resulting in acute stomach pains. ... Still it was food.'

[Near Ban Pong] 'The meals for each day were similar. Breakfast consisted of watery rice which we called porridge and tea without milk or sugar. The midday meal was again boiled rice over which was poured "jungle stew". This was chopped pumpkin, sweet potatoes and something which resembled dried grass. The final meal for the day was again rice with "jungle stew", with the addition of a "rissole". The latter consisted of boiled rice rolled into a ball, flattened and then scorched on a hot plate to brown it. There was also tea, again without milk or sugar. Sometimes "coffee" was made by grinding rice and scorching it. Hot water was poured over it and this was our coffee. Sometimes the rice was flavoured with chillies and we called it names like "Hash M'Gandi". ...

Sometimes lemon grass was infused in hot water and drunk to obtain vitamins. On other occasions we would squeeze small limes over our rice. This is where our pay became so important, even though the amount was trivial. The occasional duck egg or hand of bananas kept us alive. ...

One day we learned that Red Cross food parcels had arrived and we waited impatiently for them to be distributed, and waited, and waited. When finally they were issued we had one tenth of a parcel each.'

96

Jack Whitehead. 'In the Sonkurai camp we had bananas and were allowed to hang up bunches in our sleeping quarters to ripen, but if you upset a Jap guard he would come in and slash them down.'

Reg Parnell. *[Somewhere on the Railway, from his grandson's account]* 'They were living on rice, salt and things like snakes and turtles and anything caught in the jungle. He ate over one and a half tons of dried rice with husks along with live maggots and beetles and he has vowed never to eat any more rice.'

Eric Cullum. 'As part of the concert party, I managed to escape some of the daily work so that we could rehearse. When the Japs found out, I was sent to work in the cookhouse and this was where I mostly stayed. I ended up as a pastry cook. We made bread and tarts in tins made by tinsmiths and also kneaded rice to be moulded into cups and bowls which were baked or deep fried to act as vessels to hold scrambled egg etc.'

Dick Osborne. 'When rice was being served to prisoners it was slopped from the huge caldrons, very hot, into smaller 5 gallon drums to take to each group of men and from there into their individual eating containers. As the last man got served a rat was found in the bottom of the drum. We didn't know it was there till the can was empty. The last few men refused to eat their rice, but most had already consumed theirs. We didn't mind eating snakes but not rats.'

Reggie Griffin.*[In Osaka, 1943]* 'Rumours about Red Cross boxes coming into camp. At last the rumour has come true. 30th November we all got a box each containing 1 pkt sugar ½lb, 1 lb tin of milk, ½lb cheese, four tins butter 3 ozs, 1 pkt raisins 15 ozs, 2 tins Prem 12 ozs, 1 tin corned beef 12 ozs, 1 tin salmon 7 ozs, 1 tin coffee 4 ozs, 1 tin Rose Mill P té 6 ozs, 5 pkts cigs, 2 toilet soap, 2 pkts chewing gum, 2 bars chocolate 8 ozs and 1 tin jam 6 ozs. Dec 8th had earthquake.

On Xmas Eve got another box, also two oranges and ten cookies. Xmas Day sweet barley pap, two bread rolls, Dinner sweet beans, veg hash, one loaf and a half of bread, 2 sweet buns, nine more cookies and fish for tea. One day's holiday that was Xmas Day.'

The impression given here that Reggie received a whole parcel to himself is very unlikely to have been true. Bill Garrod says they had one between 14 men in 1943 before they went to Japan, and one between two men on November 1944 and again in December 1944. Fred Hoskins refers to one between ten men. Many Red Cross parcels were apparently commandeered by the Japanese.

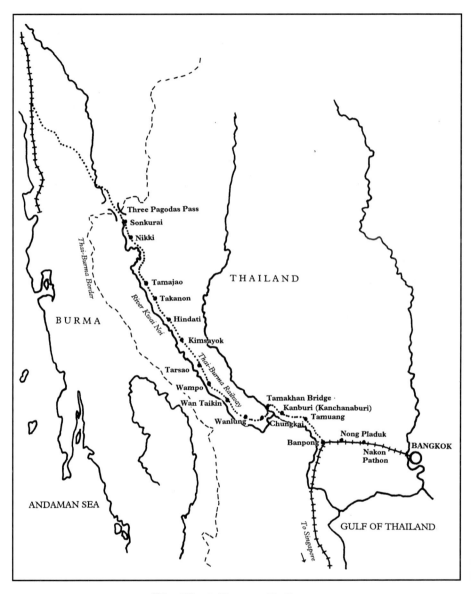

The Thai-Burma Railway
Showing only the camps named in this book – there were many others.

98

The Thai-Burma Railway

In June 1942 the Japanese began to construct a railway from Thailand [Siam] to Burma to provide a supply-line for their troops fighting on the Burma front. They began moving prisoners out of Changi up country to new camps, to provide slave labour for this giant undertaking. Ronald Searle said in his account: 'If the men who died building it were laid end to end, they would roughly cover the 273 miles of track they built...'

The first camp was at Nong Pladuk near Ban Pong. As the railway progressed, so camps were established further north, and further from the supply base for food and medication.

Fred Hoskins. 'The Japanese said we were to go up country to Thailand to a healthier camp where conditions would be much better for us. We would even have a piano. This was about June 1942 and we had much to learn about the Japanese mind. The first party to go included many of my friends and, although still weak from dysentery, I asked to be included. I didn't want to be left behind.

... Early in the morning we collected our few possessions and climbed into lorries which took us to the railway station. There we found a goods train waiting for us. It consisted of closed-in metal trucks, each with a central door and about forty of us were herded into each. There was no room to move and inside it was hot. Some of us lay on the floor and others huddled down, trying to avoid getting army boots in the face. We travelled north in this fashion for five days with occasional night halts for food. In the tropical sun, the truck was like an oven and we took it in turns to get near the door. Those with dysentery would climb out on to the buffers to relieve themselves.

... Occasionally the train would stop for more logs and water and the guards would sometimes allow us to get out of the trucks while this was being done. There was nowhere to escape to. Through the central door we could glimpse the countryside through which we were passing. We saw an elephant shifting trees with its trunk and a large snake gliding through the undergrowth. But the heat in the truck was unbearable. In the distant sky I saw a small black cloud drifting towards us and as it moved overhead it rained briefly – oh blessed relief!

On the fifth day the train stopped at the village of Ban Pong alongside a river. We got out, dirty and tired. We were formed up in columns of four rows and marched off under guard. We were going to our new camp. There was a shock awaiting us. The bamboo and atap huts stood in a foot of water and we had to wade to our bed spaces. Along each side of the hut were horizontal bamboo canes on which we had to sleep; each of us had two feet of space....

We were then marched off a mile or so to a banana plantation at a place called Nong Pladuk. This we learned was to be our camp. It was alongside a railway line. Each day we had to march from Ban Pong to Nong Pladuk to construct the huts we were to live in... Gradually it emerged that we were to build a railway line from this point to Burma, connecting with a place called Ye. Our education in a new way of life was beginning.'

Many hundreds of prisoners were to take this journey in similar conditions. Beyond Ban Pong the up-country camps were reached by marching.

Charlie Frost. 'I was among 30 men sent to the station. We were packed into steel trucks and the door slammed on us, leaving us suffocating in the heat. We travelled all day and in the evening were allowed out and given a bowl of rice after we had filled the train engines with water and loaded wood for fuel. After 4 days travelling we arrived at base camp at Nong Pladuk.
... Later we moved up the Burma Siam Railway. It was all marching. It wasn't easy to get laden boats up the River Kwai against the flow. The bridge over the River Kwai *[Tamakhan Bridge]* had already been completed.'

Bill Garrod. '750 men made up a trainload. We were put into goods wagons – 31 in each. We quickly learnt Japanese numbering as we had to parade before embarking. We spent four days travelling; by day it was like an oven, by night we froze. There were some stops for water and rice. For the toilet, you hung over the side with two friends hanging onto you. The first proper stop was at Ban Pong. We slept in atap huts a foot deep in water on wooden slats. Next stop Chungkai.'

Jack Whitehead. 'In August 1942 we left for Thailand. We were crowded into a cattle-truck for five days and nights. These were made of metal and you couldn't touch the sides for heat. The floors became awash with sewage, as we were never allowed out at all. Some men did jump out and dashed into the jungle, but were never seen again.'

Reggie Griffin. 'The next day we had to leave Changi and Singapore to go up Thailand to help the rest of the boys to build the railway through Thailand to Burma. We went in covered trucks, 25 in one. The first place we stopped at in Thailand was called Banpong; there they gave us ten bananas each. We got off the main line and got in open trucks to get on the line that the boys had already made. This was about 30 miles; here we got off the train, sleeping out in the open. Canton Buri *[Kanburi]* it was lovely weather for two days and nights, then it rained the rest of the time, so you can tell what we were like with no tents or anything to get in out of the rain ... stopped there for ten

A train for transporting PoWs to the railway camps

Reggie Griffin was not sent up country until March 1943. After that he was in and out of various camps.

days, then moved about 67 kilos. This place was called Wampo South. Here we had one tent to 100 men. Stopped here about fourteen days, then moved up to Torso *[Tarsao]*, that was another 17 kilos. Stopped there two days then on to Takanon where we had to start making the line. Our biggest job here was blasting the side of a mountain down; this was done by hammers and chisels and blasting it down into the river. All the camps we had were beside the river to get drinking water. This camp was where we lost a lot of the boys with cholera. Nine and ten were burnt for five or six days. We finished work here and moved another 15 kilos up to Cameron Park ...'

Dick Osborne. '... Chungkai. This was where we started building The Railway. I was making embankments and cuttings. We worked in gangs of 100 men, but at the end of a week, there were only about 80 – some had died, others were ill. Many had dysentery or cerebral malaria. Private Giles of the Royal Norfolks was the first man in the cemetery there.

The reduced working party had to finish their allotted stint regardless. Each stretch of railway was about 5 km. When you had finished the work in one place, you leap-frogged the gangs in between to start a new stretch in another camp up river.'

101

Bill Garrod describes the work on Wampo viaduct, one of the most difficult construction jobs on the railway. As a builder he was better able to cope with the work than many, and was good at finding solutions to problems.

Bill Garrod. *[At Chungkai]* 'Here we were put to work building tracks and embankments. As a builder I found the work easier than those who had done sedentary jobs at home.

We were making a viaduct at Wampo, 70ft above the river. There was a jutting rock in the way. Instead of tunnelling they blew a wedge off the side, then built a flimsy structure to take the rails. This was Wampo Bridge. It was made in several levels. The bottom one had huge timbers 15 inches square, which had to be cut in the forest with a crosscut saw, axes and adzes. Then we had to make an auger hole for an iron rod. The men who had never used an auger often made the hole at the wrong angle and they got the auger up the backside. These huge timbers were dragged over rough ground by elephants – but what an elephant couldn't pull, we had to carry. Teams of 30 men were placed 15 on either side of the huge log with smaller timber at right angles underneath. Then you and your opposite number had to lift together and shuffle along. If someone stumbled in a hole you got all the weight. Eventually each massive log was dragged to a raft on the river.

At each stage of building, the wooden frame had to be levelled with stones and concrete basketed up from a barge in the river. Then the stanchions for the next stage could be put in. The top level held the rails and there was very little room to work. When officials came to inspect the work, they just pushed the prisoners off – to fall in the river. You soon learned to hang on to the rail or a stanchion as they approached.

When you had finished one section, you leap-frogged another group. You went about 30 miles further on and started work all over again.'

Dick Langley. 'Kanburi camp contained thousands of prisoners, a huge camp which eventually became a sort of hospital. This is where I started work on the railway. I moved on to Tamakhan Bridge and to Chungkai, a reasonable camp.

Work on Wampo viaduct was soul-destroying effort with hammer and chisel. Every morning you looked round to see who was still alive next to you. Here we had cholera whose victims died very quickly. In the monsoon, corpses were floating down the river and that was where we had to wash.

At Tarsao many trees had already been cut down, but the next working party had to make railway sleepers out of the stumps. We were working bare-footed. I considered myself lucky to have picked up an Australian hat in Singapore which kept the sun off my head. Tarsao was more civilised than some camps and there was no bridge work to be done'

102

Prisoners working on the Tamakhan Bridge

Reg Bullard. 'From there *[Kanburi]* to Wampo to slog for 25 hours shifts on bridgework, carrying baulks of timber onto the wooden supports. A very tricky and dangerous place as the river was below. After finishing this job it was on the move again on foot through the mud, water and jungle to the camp at Tarsao. As this camp was just in tatters and waterlogged we pushed on again to a camp known as Takanon, which was a tented camp with bamboo structures for cookhouse and the hospital area. G. Hardiment died here in November 1943.

The work here was getting ballast from the river and rock blasting to level for the track-laying and also cutting down trees for the railway engines.

The camps provided the most basic shelter for the labour force. Fred Hoskins describes the actual building of their camp at Nong Pladuk.

Fred Hoskins. 'Some of us were issued with wooden yokes with a basket on each end. Others had chunkels. We had to take down the banana trees and level the ground. The soil for levelling was carried in the baskets. At the end of each day we returned to Ban Pong, our shoulders raw and blistered as

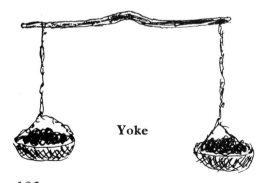

Yoke

103

a result of the unaccustomed heavy work in the tropical sun. Sometimes we disturbed snakes and scorpions. The next day we changed over jobs, the basket-carriers of the previous day now using chunkels under the watchful eyes of the guards who always carried their rifles with fixed bayonets.

Chunkel

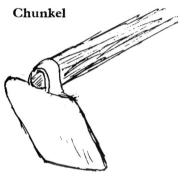

We learned the hated word "Speedo" shouted by a guard and often followed by a blow. We learned ways to save our strength. We walked more slowly or stopped work when the guard was not looking. We put less soil in the baskets ... Slowly the camp was built. The huts were wood-framed with bamboo matting sides and holes cut for windows. The roofs were made of atap, which made it look as if it had been thatched. The whole was raised off the ground two or three feet. Railway sleepers were used to make steps up to the entrance. Each hut was intended to hold two or three hundred men. There were six, forming a U shape and a cookhouse, Japanese headquarters and a guardroom near the gate. All were of similar construction and the camp was enclosed by a high bamboo fence. Each man was allowed only two feet of space.

Interior of hospital hut at Kanchanaburi

The cookhouse was supplied with large cast-iron pans or "dobies" which were set on baked mud bricks and heated by wood fires underneath. A wood-collecting party would leave the camp daily, escorted by a Japanese guard, and this sometimes led to trouble with the local Thais. From the remnants of the wood from the building of the huts, some of us made simple beds until

104

stopped by the guards. Mine consisted of three removable planks in a framework over which I laid my blanket. The planks were removable to enable me to clean out the bugs which rapidly infested all huts. One night I counted 97, which I removed as they crawled over me. They gave off a pungent smell when crushed.'

Jack Whitehead also worked on the making of this camp. Jack was part of the leading group doing preliminary work all along the course of the railway. They didn't stay long in each place before going on to another camp.

Jack Whitehead. 'I was on the hammer and chisel job. The hammer weighed 14 lb and you often missed the chisel when you were hammering, especially in monsoon rain. The rain filled the hole you were making and at the next hammer blow you got a burst of water in the face. Later the Japs used gelignite and the POW's had to clear the rubble with their hands. You kept telling yourself it couldn't go on for ever. Some gave up straight away and died.

Some of the camps were very primitive. In one tented camp, our living quarters were above a muddy, slippery 6-foot slope to the ground below. In the rainy season you had difficulty in standing up in the mud and once you had gone down the slope you couldn't get back up again. Then you were beaten – by bamboo, chisel, spade or shovel until you did get up.'

Despite being a medical orderly, Harry Cassidy was sent out on working parties.

Harry Cassidy. 'We took donkey-carts (no donkeys, but men in the shafts) to load up sacks of rice. When we got back to the camp the Japs searched the men but not the carts, so we sometimes managed to acquire an egg or a banana!'

The most northerly camp was Sonkurai, just south of Three Pagodas Pass; this was where the railway was joined on to the track from Burma.

Busty Rudd. 'I remember being in Tamuang, Kanchanaburi, Chungkai, Takanon – working on the bridge, Wampo viaduct, Tarsao, Kimbayok, Tamajao, Nikki and Sonkurai. This last was a cholera camp. I saw 500 men burnt on funeral pyres.

Reggie Griffin and I were mates on the Railway. In Sonkurai Reggie went out of his mind with cerebral malaria. The Jap guards took him out into the jungle and left him there to die, their standard treatment for this condition. *[Busty and some other POWs went to see him every night and gave him drinks and tablets, which they had to force down his throat. They had stolen the tablets from Jap quarters in the camp].*

105

I remember the hard work making embankments, digging out holes and loading spoil onto stretchers of rice sacks and bamboo poles. Each hole was 3–4ft across and of the same depth. If the hole was not completed at the end of a day's graft there was no going back to camp until it was done. Next day, the size of the hole demanded was even bigger.

After the Railway was completed we returned from Sonkurai by train. As we went over Wampo Viaduct it creaked all the way. As the viaduct was built earlier on, it had been sabotaged by the prisoners. We used to put trees on the embankments when we weren't being observed and cover them up with soil, so that in time they would rot and derail the train.'

Charlie Frost. 'We had got well on the way towards Three Pagodas Pass and by that time we were really just skeletons. Our job was to carry 1cwt sacks of rice from the boats over a wet, steep bank. You often slipped and fell.

Having been a farm worker I could manage the task pretty well, but the city boys weren't used to hard work and often fell and had to be helped. Our job inland was to cut hardwood for sleepers and that meant felling sizeable trees with a peculiarly shaped Jap saw, which had to be pulled towards you.'

Jack Whitehead. 'In November 1943, the Railway was completed and our work was just cleaning up the camps and repairing the railway after bombing by the Allies. I left Thailand in February 1944. By March 1944, we were all back in Singapore for a rest period. That meant a bit less work.'

George Parnell. *[From his grandson's account]* 'When the Railway was finished the prisoners went into the jungle, cutting down trees for firewood which was fuel for the engines as there was no coal; it was very hard work as temperatures rose to 120°F in the shade. During the latter part of the war he was forced to cut sidings for the trains as the Japs were in retreat.'

Dick Osborne. In 1944 at Tamakhan *[the Bridge over the River Kwai]* the Railway was finished and I was there when the bridge was bombed. I still get nightmares.

Some time in 1944, I left Chungkai and went to Kanburi to work on bridges etc. One afternoon we were bombed by Allied planes and more damage was done to the bridges. Some of our chaps were killed and our huts were set on fire. We heard some of the Japs were killed as well.

Moving on from this camp, we found ourselves in a New Camp, which was a big change from what we were used to. There were new wooden huts and roads already made – a big change. We could not understand why this Camp was built, but it seemed to be a propaganda show camp and a cover-up for the treatment we had received.'

Punishment

The very life the prisoners led was punishment enough, but there were extra penalties for certain types of misbehaviour.

Harry Cassidy. 'I remember one group punishment. We were made to stand without water for 4 hours near an apple tree. The guard picked several and crunched them loudly in front of us. ...

When you met a Jap you had to bow and say 'Kooway'. If you didn't see them you got a heavy cupped hand over your ear and some men had burst eardrums.'

Charlie Frost. 'Someone stole one of the tools so as a punishment we all had to stand outside the guard room all day in the sun for a week. You had not to move, or you got a stick in the back. You had no water, so several collapsed. There were eight of us to start with, but only three or four survived. When the punishment ended they were so dehydrated they could hardly eat or walk. The man who had taken the tool was eventually caught and suffered the same fate.'

Eric Cullum. 'I was always one for acting and singing. I was a chorus girl in *Me and My Girl*. One of my friends was a PoW acting as batman to a Jap officer, who had a guitar. This he was persuaded to lend to a concert party, but it was returned with a broken string. I got beaten across the head four or five times and was deaf for two days. I later managed to explain that I was not the one who broke the string and the Jap gave me ten cigarettes. ...

There was one particularly nasty Korean in the Jap kitchen. He was called Carbody and took delight in pouring hot soup over my hands as I held my officer's bowl. I complained and his officer went and slapped the Korean.'

Reggie Griffin. 'As I left Singapore at the start of my time on the Siam-Burma Railway our lorry passed heads cut off and stuck on gateposts. There were six or seven different ones every day. If they wanted a head they had it – anyone, any nationality.'

Dick Osborne. 'For quite trivial misdeeds we would be put into bamboo cages, in which you could neither stand nor lie stretched out. You could only crouch inside. We were left in these cages in full sun for several days.

I also heard about, but did not witness, the "water punishment". Men were forced to drink and drink, then a Jap jumped on to his belly.'

Bertie Boyce. 'Many chaps were given rough treatment. A Jap would jump on a man's stomach and many had burst stomachs. Some even had water forced down their throats; tied up in the heat of the day, shut in small boxes. All the time the Medical Officers did what they could with hardly anything, whilst the Padres held services and communion, but this did not give much comfort.'

Fred Hoskins tells how this bad treatment on one occasion led to a strike.

Fred Hoskins. 'Life on the railway continued day after day and beatings were frequent. One day a man was taken away by a Japanese engineer and after some time of absence members of the work party went to see where he was. They found him on the ground being jumped on by the engineer, who had been drinking heated sake, a distillation of fermented rice. It was the last straw and the Japanese had been warned by our Commanding Officer, Major S.

The next morning, the bugle sounded the parade call for work, but with rapidly beating hearts we stayed in our huts, refusing to work, and so began the terrifying episode of our strike. The thin high-pitched voice of Ichi Kura could be heard. Then the officers were ordered to one part of the camp while we had to parade in another, in a long line facing the front. An alarm call by the Japanese brought in from outside a large body of Japanese troops who came running in, their chin straps below their chins and rifles held ready with fixed bayonets. They lined up facing us while the officers were led off behind some trees. The cookhouse fires were put out.

A Japanese sergeant, carrying a curved black stick instead of the usual sword and accompanied by guards and the interpreter, walked along the line. "Why you no go work?" he demanded followed by a slash of the stick. We felt that this could be the end as we looked at the threatening rifles opposite.

"Can I go to the latrines, Staff?" a voice said urgently behind me.

"No! Stay where you are!' The Japanese stood in front of me and repeated his question. "Where are our officers?" I asked.

108

"You have no officers!" and he passed along the line.

Eventually it was agreed that if we went back to work the beatings would cease, but for the officers, they had to be punished. They were to stand to attention facing the tropical sun for one month! We went to work with a feeling of helplessness as they stood in front of a hut for the rest of the day. It so happened that one of the officers had been out of the camp collecting rice supplies from Ban Pong. On his return he demanded to be allowed to join his brother officers. This was refused as he had not actually taken part in the strike. The Japanese Camp Commander sent him away with the words "Tomorrow, tomorrow." Just after midnight the British officer again demanded to see the Japanese Commanding Officer and this time the officers were released from their punishment. Within a few days the beatings recommenced.'

Charlie Frost. *At Nong Pladuk* 'Tools were missing. These had been stolen by the previous group, but our group had the punishment. We had to stand in the broiling sun outside the guardroom for seven days and nights without moving at all and without water or food. Two out of three died. Those three or four of us who were left standing at the end had to be helped to walk back to our huts. We were given food and drink, but we could hardly swallow it – but our friends could!

Once I was put to work as striker for a Jap blacksmith making sack needles. The Jap was holding a red hot chisel to make an eye in the needle and I was not hitting hard enough. The blacksmith said "More squashee" so finally I hit really hard and broke the end off the chisel. The blacksmith chased me, brandishing the red hot stump to stab me – I was nearly naked – but he couldn't catch me.

We were unloading railway lines from a truck. Nearby was another old wagon with some natives in it, who looked nearly dead. We went to help them, but were ordered to dig a grave and unload the natives into it. But they were not dead and some of them sat up. When we pointed this out to the Jap guards, they just took shovels and chopped their heads off and said, "Now get on and bury them."'

Disease and Injury

In the beginning medical resources, such as they were, had to be applied to the injuries resulting from the fighting before the surrender. But the prisoners soon began to suffer from a variety of diseases: some, like malaria and Dengue fever, were native to the area and others resulted from the insanitary conditions in the camps. As time wore on, vitamin deficiencies produced beri-beri and other ailments connected with malnutrition. Ulcers and ringworm, fleas and lice added to the multiple discomforts of prison life. Malaria and dysentery were rife and killed many, but the disease most feared, by prisoners and Japanese alike, was cholera.

Harry Cassidy. *Harry had ulcerated legs, like so many of his companions, and the flies got on them. They used to pack them with mud and let the sun bake it hard. When it eventually wore off the ulcers seemed smaller.*

Charlie Frost. 'During my time in Changi I reported to the British MO with ingrowing toe nails. The doctor grabbed a pair of forceps and wrenched it off. There were no anaesthetics. I didn't show the other foot! Later I was very ill with pneumonia and lost consciousness. I woke to find myself under a blanket being taken out feet first.'

Bill Garrod. *When he was in Wan Lung,* 'If you became really sick or badly injured you either died or were sent down river by barge to Chungkai, or Kanburi or Tarsao but many died on the way. I had beri-beri and reached Tamajo where there was a cholera epidemic. I didn't catch it, but was sent to Takanon where there were some 5th Norfolks.'

Fred Hoskins. 'This diet was deficient in vitamins and beri-beri became a problem. If the flesh was pressed, the dent took a long time to disappear. Those worst affected swelled up and then died, becoming at the time of death skin over bones. A man's teeth and gums could be seen outlined in his cheeks and you could count his ribs.'

Jack Whitehead. 'I was always getting malaria. I had no dysentery, but a bit of beri-beri. You couldn't wash except in the river and that's where the cholera came from. You caught it by mouth. The Japs shot anyone they saw putting his head under water.

The only hope for cholera cases was a saline drip. There were no needles, but one of the medical orderlies made a needle out of bamboo.'

Dick Osborne. 'Wan Tai Kin was where I first got sick. About a year later I was returned to the hospital camp at Chungkai. By that time I had severe beri-beri, ulcers on my legs, Dengue fever and scabies. I never had malaria or dysentery and put that down to the fact that I refused to eat any food on which I had seen a fly land. I had bugs and lice and once went delirious when I was bitten on the face by a bug. The only treatment I had in the so-called hospital was an allocation of rice husks, which made the beri-beri better.

During monsoons, the river flowed very fast and was warm. If you went in, it warmed you up and the fish cleaned up your sores for you...

In a New Camp. 'I stayed there for a few months and during that time I was asked if I would give blood to a very sick man. It was all very crude. I remember lying on a bamboo bed with the Australian recipient beside me ... I had yellow jaundice in this last camp.'

Bertie Perkins. *Told by his wife, Gladys.* 'He said he had to walk between all the camps he went to on the Railway. He had amoebic dysentery and was constantly dropping out of line to relieve himself or from fatigue. He had to be goaded and dragged along to the next camp by his mates. He worked burying prisoners who had died, often several in one day.'

Dick Langley. 'From Tarsao I went back to Kanburi. At that time I was suffering from amoebic dysentery, malaria, Dengue fever, dry beri-beri and leg ulcers. I remember Dr de Wardener treating me there. The leg ulcers miraculously healed; some other men had them treated with maggots. Ulcers were the main reason for amputations.'

Reg Bullard. *At Takanon.* 'This was not a very good camp healthwise. Cholera, dysentery and malaria ravaged the camp at the monsoon time as the river overflowed causing disease. Bad memories here of so many deaths, graves had to be dug and pyres to be made for the boys that died of cholera. All this work had to be done by the sick. We did get some supplies for malaria, quinine in powder form that was disgusting to taste but helped. I had malaria, dysentery and did get a jab against cholera. It was on 11 October 1943, I buried Reggie Brown, a workmate from Sparham...'

Later. 'At this time, I had a touch of tropical ringworm, and also got a series of boils, but kept plodding along.'

Eric Dack. 'I was taken ill with shingles and never got much rest from the pain for a fortnight and the sweat ran down my body into the sores. I could get no relief; no drugs were available to treat this condition. I no sooner felt I was getting over this when I got yellow jaundice and felt pretty rough.

It was about this time I received a letter from home. I thought this would

111

cheer me up. When I read it, Mother had written to tell me Lily *[his fiancée]* was being married. She had written the letter on the very day she was married, and of course I felt it and it didn't do me any good. I laid in the cell and felt the bottom had dropped out of my world.'

Fred Hoskins. 'We now found we had another problem – body lice. Regularly on the occasion of 'yasume' *[rest day]* we would boil such clothing and blankets as we had for a minimum of twenty minutes and this way we kept it under control. ... Flies too were an abomination. ...Working on the railway often resulted in skin damage to arms and legs, and dozens of flies would be attracted to the sore places. Dreadful ulcers then developed, the flesh melting away and leaving the bone exposed. The only treatment then was for the arm or leg to be amputated. In one hut there were about two hundred men with amputated limbs and the stench was sickening. We were able to buy small round patches of paper with tar on them which, if applied to the damaged area immediately, kept the flies off and reduced the risk of infection.'

Bertie Boyce. 'Chloroform and morphine were in short supply but the Japanese refused many requests from the Medical officers to give them anything. It was a dreadful situation for them trying to give comfort and such for any one. They made do with what could be found, sometimes using bamboo for drips; the saline solution I think was sea water, for we had no salt. There were several amputations as many with wounds, legs and arms, were now gangrenous. Luckily my arm did heal enough to escape that. There was some blindness as well. Much of this was lack of vitamins. All kinds of plants we used to provide a drug, vitamin, etc. We found the rice husk had some good vitamins. The rice itself was no good as it just swelled us up with water, so we had what we called rice bellies....

There was chap from Nottingham I knew who was in Changi jail. He got a nasty head wound that was so bad he had to be kept out of the way of any Japanese in case he was struck on the head which was something they enjoyed doing. Doctor Taylor, a Medical officer, who had worked in a top London hospital did an operation on this chap using what he could. He managed to even get some chloroform and he took a bit of bone from this chap's leg and grafted into the wound in his head. I did not see his head wound but it is a fact that it was nasty and a small stone could be put into it. This chap made it home and he passed away a few years ago. This was really a miracle. There were many life saving things done by the Medical officers who had to perform in dreadful conditions. Those who had operations with not enough chloroform were very brave and had complete trust in the Medical Officers.'

D. *[the famous Australian surgeon, Weary Dunlop]* was the medical officer and one day, as they examined my hand, an orderly placed a dish under it and cut quickly across the palm with a scalpel. Taken by surprise, I yelled at the sudden pain of it, but the deed was done. The wound was then drained and stuffed with an entire bandage. Each day, the bandage was withdrawn, a pair of tongs inserted in the hole and jerked open to continue the draining, with the same agonising effect. This continued for about three days and an oiled bandage used as the first bandages tended to stick on the raw wound.

Slowly it improved. The bandages were scarce and so were boiled and re-used time and again, becoming very discoloured but sterile. The wound in my thigh seemed to be responding to treatment. Then one day, I began to feel dizzy and found I was sitting in my own blood, the wound having opened up again. A further operation became necessary with again the cotton wool pad over my mouth and chloroform and ether. A fragment of cloth from my trousers and a piece of metal were found by probing and removed. From then on my leg began to heal properly.'

The operating theatre at Nakon Pathon

Ingenuity

In the extreme conditions of the camps the men's genius for improvisation flourished. Stealing food was an accepted and necessary way of supplementing supplies, though not many managed to do it on the scale of Joe Mason.

Joe Mason. *Retold by his son, Fred.* 'One day they were all lined up at Changi camp and the guards asked for volunteers who had experience of waiting at table. Some Jap dignitaries were coming to a meal. Joe, like everyone else in the army, didn't believe in volunteering for anything but this time he did. He knew what he was doing. He had not, of course, done any waiting. Dad was 5'6" tall and weighed only 7 stone at this time. He borrowed a shirt from a prisoner who was very tall and broad. When he returned from his mission the huge shirt was bulging all round with stolen food. There was enough food for the whole hut for several days.'

Basic army skills, plus the expertise of those who had other civilian training, enabled them to perform minor miracles with the equipment to hand.

Fred Hoskins. 'A large circular hole was dug in the centre of the 'padang' or parade ground which soon filled with water. A bucket suspended from a beam and weighted at the opposite end was fixed at the edge and we drew our water from there. It was satisfactory, but the bank soon became muddy and slippery from spilled water. Most of us acquired an empty four-gallon petrol tin which we filled with water and left in the sun all day. At the end of the day's work we had a can of really warm water for washing off the day's grime and sweat. Only very rarely were we issued with soap. ... Three times I had all my hair taken off by the camp barber as it was easier to keep clean and many others did likewise. We had one small issue of toilet paper during the whole time and this was poor quality, showing the straw in it. We used it for keeping the accounts for the working parties.

A water tower was constructed next to the cookhouse and Mechanics Sergeant Major H. and Sergeant Major O'S. were responsible for the petrol engine which pumped the water up to the tank... They had a small petrol stove and, using petrol from the pump, were able to fry the occasional duck egg. ... Occasionally a duck from the neighbouring kampong might waddle through the bamboo fence, upon which a large bamboo basket would be put over it to keep it there until it laid an egg, whereupon it was released. If a duck was eaten, it was essential to get rid of every trace of feathers.'

Harry Cassidy. *In Java.* 'I was in Java for 3½ years moving from camp to camp. During that time we had no change of clothing. Our shoes wore out and a Dutchman made sandals with a wooden sole and a toe strap. We shaved with pieces of broken glass.'

Similar sandals were issued to Fred Hoskins in Nong Pladuk.

Fred Hoskins. 'Our boots had worn out and we were given one-piece wooden clogs which had a toe-strap made of old bicycle tyre. While walking with these I kicked one against my shin. A small ulcer developed, but by treating it with neat carbolic acid it slowly went.

When the monsoon rains came, some men made themselves hats by cutting along the seams of old rice sacks and turning up the edges. They were also useful as a protection from the glare and heat of the sun. The Japanese stopped this owing to the shortage of rice sacks....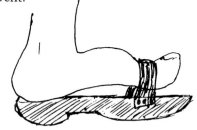

An officer set up a dental centre giving such treatment as his limited resources permitted. Tooth powder was made from ground chalk. One day a Japanese soldier with toothache asked for treatment. He was told to get cocaine and in due course returned with this. The officer filled the syringe with water which he injected and then proceeded with the extraction, telling the Japanese afterwards that the pain was caused by poor quality Japanese cocaine!

It was found that by patiently scraping paper from an old exercise book with a razor blade, two thin pieces of paper could be obtained and these could be used as cigarette paper. Cigarette rolling machines were made from pieces of canvas and wood and the cigarettes stuck down with sticky rice water. Many of those who had lost limbs did this and so earned some money selling ready-made cigarettes to their friends. Old exercise books were therefore in great demand and bibles were particularly popular as usually the paper was already thin. I bought a pipe from Private B and boiled it to sterilise it. ... We called the tobacco by various names such as Hag's Bush or Sheik's Beard. I used a chipped magnifying glass for lighting the pipe. ... Early on we bought native cigarettes rolled in a piece of banana leaf and tied round with a piece of red cotton. We found they were unsmokeable unless we removed the banana leaf and re-rolled them in paper.

The Japanese issued fly swats. These were bamboo sticks with a flap of rubber at one end. They said they would pay a day's wage for a bamboo container filled with dead flies.... Soon this became a new way of earning money by those too ill to work...they received no pay and the food provided was deficient in the essential vitamins. A frame of bamboo sticks was constructed like a miniature house with sloping roof and a piece of mosquito net draped over it, leaving a gap around the base of about half an inch. Food was placed underneath and flies zoomed in through the gap and then flew up and were trapped. Soon the whole frame would be buzzing.

The frame was then immersed in water and the flies drowned. They were then spread out in the sun to dry and duly handed in to the Japanese for payment. One sick man could look after three or four traps. The flies were then taken to the incinerator for burning, under escort of a guard but sometimes rescued for use a second time! ...'

[On the Burma railway] 'It was hot and tiring work unloading heavy equipment and large bales of cotton waste. We systematically did small acts of sabotage such as treading parts of machinery into the ground. Bales of cotton waste were pushed from the tops of stacks to fall heavily on metal trolleys which buckled and became useless.'

Fred also records that at Nong Pladuk they had their own system of paper money.

'Each pay day our Commanding Officer received our pay in large denomination Thai notes which obviously couldn't be divided among the men. We therefore devised our own currency for circulation within the camp. This consisted of squares of cardboard each measuring about three quarters of an inch. They were stamped 5c, 10c and 15cents in green or red ink. They couldn't be counterfeited because no one else had cardboard or ink.

The cardboard money was accepted by the Thais in the camp. When they had enough, they would exchange them for the large denomination notes that circulated outside the camp. We also had some Thai coins and one dollar notes.'

Harry Cassidy. *His teeth rotted on the rice diet in Java and* 'Corporal Hathaway made me a plate from a billy-can.'

The Thai people were also capable of quick-thinking ingenuity when required. Ted Brown's widow recalls his experience.

Ted Brown. 'Ted had been blinded by beri-beri as a FEPOW on the Burma-Siam railway. Of course he couldn't join the construction parties, but used to go into the jungle, led by a friendly Thai villager, to negotiate for eggs or vegetables to supplement the prisoners' diet. As he stood in the Thai's house, talking to his wife, a child rushed in shouting "Nippon!"

If he had been found by a Japanese soldier Ted would certainly have been shot dead as this kind of trading was forbidden. With very quick thought, the Thai woman pushed him onto a bed and covered him up, then went to the door and, blocking the doorway, told the Jap guard, "Don't come in. There is a case of typhoid here!" The Jap fled. Illness of any kind seemed to terrify them. This action saved Ted's life.

Ted suffered terrible nightmares until the day he died. He never regained his sight.'

Eric Dack. 'Before I went into *[Changi]* Jail I was able to get a supply of wool by raiding a store at the end of the day's work, and wrapping the scarves around my waist, then my old shirt went over the top. I was jolly uncomfortable by the time I got to camp, plus the fact the Japs might have thought I had put on some weight, or was hiding something. I pulled the wool out and made balls from it, then with the aid of wire produced some needles for knitting socks. After trial and error I was able to turn the heel and graft the toes. Being able to graft became useful one day when one of the officers, Capt. M. Keith had some hose, which was not long enough for him. He had heard what I was able to do. He was over six feet tall and wanted these lengthened. I cut through the hose, picked up the stitches and knitted the odd wool so it was covered when the top was turned over.'

Concerts and pantomimes provided entertainment, especially at Christmas. These were more frequent in Changi Camp than in the smaller up-country camps, and the Australians seem to have been star performers. Men playing the female parts were particularly popular.

Reggie Griffin. 'On the 20th Dec. [1942] we had a concert called the Shoe Shine Shokies. ... On Christmas Eve we had some carol singing. ...On Xmas night we had a good pantomime called "Jack and the Beanstalk."'

Fred Hoskins. 'In the days preceding Christmas, the cookhouse would save some of our rations so that on the day, a better meal could be served. The day would be allowed as a holiday and a concert arranged on a makeshift stage of earth which had been banked up. Great ingenuity was used in devising grass skirts for 'ladies' and the acts were very varied. The concert would be held in the evening and I remember that on one occasion, as the concert came to an end, we spontaneously sang the National Anthem to the great annoyance of the Japanese, and Ichi Kura's voice could be heard shouting "Stopo – stopo!" We put the name Prince of Wales above the stage in large letters in the hope that any allied aircraft would see it and realise it was a Prisoner of War camp. The Japanese made us take it down.'

Reg Bullard. 'Now as it was getting close to Christmas 1943 some sports were held in cooperation with the Officers and the Jap Commandant. This was done to help the funds of the hospital. As Xmas arrived, a pantomime was held at the Beach Pavilion made by the boys. This was known as "Babes in Thailand" played by the officers and some of the boys and it was a very good show. The National Anthem and the Dutch Anthem were played at the end of the show.'

News from the Outside World

Both sending and receiving information was made very difficult by the Japanese right from the start of the captivity.

Harry Cassidy. 'We were told we could write notes home of no more than 25 words – but as soon as they were collected up, someone saw them being burnt.'

News of all kinds was anxiously sought by the prisoners. Letters from home were slow to get through, but when they did arrive they were read many times.

Reggie Griffin. 'Well today I received my first letter, the 18th March 1943...'

Fred Hoskins. 'In the early days when the Japanese were advancing through Burma, they would give us the occasional newspaper, *The Sinon Times*. These were printed in English and were basically propaganda and told of Japanese advances on all fronts. Some told incredible stories of Japanese bravery, such as the Japanese pilot who attacked an Allied ship. When he was out of ammunition, he flew low and, with his sword, severed the head of the ship's captain as he stood on the bridge! ...

Our drivers who moved between the camps would pick up news which they passed on. It was soon found, however, that news had to be kept secret and not widespread. The Japanese interpreter would wander around the camp at night listening to the men talking among themselves. We knew when the Normandy landing was made and watched the Japanese in their Headquarters looking at their maps. ...

After fifteen months, word went round that some post had arrived in the camp and it stayed in a hut unissued for many days. Eventually the Japanese were persuaded to release it. For many it brought good news, for some bad. I received a photograph of my wife with the baby son I had never seen. In a later search while we were at work, all my photographs were taken. I went to the Japanese interpreter and asked for their return. He indicated a box in which many photographs had been thrown and I was able to retrieve mine together with a copy of the New Testament which Padre Ross had given me.'

The penalties for operating secret radios were extreme, but many did exist.

Bill Garrod. *At Aome.* 'We had a secret wireless there. The man who operated it was Paul Borough of the Royal Corps of Signals. He is now a bishop in Rhodesia. His father was a bigwig in the Church at Oxford.'

Reg Bullard. 'I think it is wise to say that even in Singapore some news was passed on by the locals, but up here it always happened that after a certain person called a little news filtered out. One day I was in charge of filling the water butt that had to be treated before being used. I needed a bucket and went to a nearby hut where a few of the boys lived. They were soldering some wires in a radio set. I never mentioned this; the old saying a still tongue keeps a wise head.'

Fred Hoskins. *In 1944.* 'There was an ugly change in the mood of the Japanese who were getting more and more edgy, and from secret radios the word filtered through that their thrust towards Burma had been halted by Allied troops. The Japanese were not accustomed to these reverses.'

From Singapore to Saigon and Japan

There were some prisoners who never worked in Singapore or on the Burma railway, but went straight to Japan.

Reg Anthony. 'I was taken prisoner on arrival and was sent straight to Japan where I became a miner near Hiroshima. My job was to go a long way down into a coal or iron ore mine. At the bottom we went miles out under the sea. I had to lie on my back and use a pick to loosen the coal or ore and then scoop it up with my hands to put it onto a conveyor belt.'

Most, however, worked in Singapore or on the Burma railway, but after the completion of the railway, many prisoners were taken to Saigon (Vietnam) to work and others on the much longer journey to Japan.

Charlie Frost. 'We were put on a boat for Saigon. It was loaded with scrap metal for Japan. Because the holds were full, we prisoners lay on deck with machine guns trained on us manned by Chinese gaolers. It was better on deck

– not so hot or dark. We could see everything.

We went in convoy but lost a ship a night to submarines, probably Yanks who didn't know we were aboard. Ours was the only boat to reach Saigon, all the others were sunk. Ashore in Saigon many Yanks came over to bomb.

We were sent inland to build airstrips. As we were waiting for our rice rations Yankee planes with two engines and a double tail came over and bombed the runway. No one was killed, but we all lost our rations. We got punished for that.

We had to drill hardcore, one man with a bar and one with a hammer. You had to make a metre cube of rubble in a day, or no food. One morning, while clearing a runway at Saigon Airport, there had just been an air raid and planes were ablaze. We had to tow them off the runway. Raids went on all day.'

Bill Garrod, Busty Rudd, Reg Bullard, Reggie Griffin *and* **Jack Whitehead** *were sent on the same convoy of twelve ships to Japan. It proved a memorable journey.*

Jack Whitehead. 'In May 1944, we left Singapore in twelve transport ships, all called something Maru, with an escort of four Japanese destroyers. Of the twelve ships, all but two were sunk by US submarines. We were all battened down in the hold and were allowed out only once a day, after dark. There was more room than in the rail trucks to Thailand, but you couldn't lie down. We were sitting in sewage and sweat.

Food was handed down in five-gallon containers and was slopped into our cupped hands as we had no mess tins. This was the only time I was really afraid. Depth charges were going off all the time; there must have been masses of US subs about.

It took about three weeks to reach Japanese waters and all the way the boat never stopped. We finally landed at Osaka and were taken to a little village called Iruka to do copper mining. The mine belonged to the Mitsubishi Company. You don't go down a copper mine but along, then up. We went on a truck along a rail for about a mile on the level, then reached a sort of clearing with a shaft rising from it with a series of ladders, leading to little individual shelves.'

Reg Bullard. 'A total of 1,500 men boarded the *Osaka Maru*, but we would not be battened down, so with some more of the boys we camped out on deck. This ship was 5,000 tons and was formerly the *Liverpool Belle*. The food was disgusting. We sailed on to North Borneo and then to the harbour of Manila where we stayed for a short while for supplies and some fruit that was welcome. This was the 13 August 1944. On leaving we headed north and thought the next stop would be Formosa (Taiwan).

On 15 August 1944, we were hit by a typhoon that caused the ship to break its back. We were taken off by their destroyers. They lost some ships and their dead troops were floating in the sea. We were still heading for Formosa where we were transferred to the *Haka San Maru* a passenger ship of 17,000 tons. From there we headed to Japan but on the way the convoy was attacked by US submarines with the loss of some ships. Howsoever we reached a port called Mugi. On arrival we all had to pass through a disinfestor and also what little kit we had. After two days we boarded a train at Sumasaka bound for Osaka. Food was served at various points en route.

Arriving at Osaka we were met by the camp staff and transported by trolley bus to the camp, which was in the shipbuilding area. At least we got a hot bath and for a change some good thick soup, the best so far. Here we had good huts with blankets and good food. Had to spend about ten days learning the lingo and doing a bit of drill Jap style. After this, we started work at the Nanwa Dock Company. I had a gang of five to form a riveting gang on the cargo ships.'

Reggie Griffin *reports the same terrible storm.* 'The sea is getting very rough now, waves coming over the ship into the hold and everywhere, nowhere to sleep. The cook house was on deck and that is washed away plus the little veg we did have. This was a very bad storm; next morning there was only two more ships with us, later in the day we lost them. The boat had started leaking... Had to run aground now ... The waves still washing over the top. All we are living on now is burnt rice that has been stored on the ship for three-four months; some is mouldy but still we have to eat it.'

Bill Garrod *was also aboard.* 'From Nong Pladuk we went by train to Singapore, four days travel, then on by boat destined for Japan. It was a 6,000 ton cargo boat, the *Osaka Maru*. She was one of several ships sold as scrap to Japan before the war. Her old name was still there on a plaque in the engine room. She was the *Glasgow Belle*! 750 men boarded this ship, already loaded with a gravelly cargo of bauxite (a source of aluminium mined in Java).

Near Borneo the ship scraped her bottom on rocks, but there was no leak in the steel plate. There we put in to load Malayan latex. This rubber sap had solidified into a sheet and this was folded over and over again to make a pack about 12" x 12" x 6". The edge of the rubber made a handle and the whole pack was like a suitcase. Each prisoner had to take two of these on board.

The PoWs travelled in the stern hold, a very claustrophobic experience. You sat crouched on the floor with sweat pouring off you till the floor was awash. A hell ship.

In September 1944 the first American air-raids brought hope, but also new dangers to the prisoners. Fred Hoskins, in Nong Pladuk, was injured in the first of these raids by B24 Flying Fortresses.

Fred Hoskins. '... in the bright moonlight we could see the shapes of huge four-engined planes. ... Unable to sleep, Sergeant Major S. and I stood on the hut steps fascinated ... I saw the shape of a plane silhouetted against the moon. "Look at that one, Joe!" I said and then we heard the tearing screech of a bomb as it came down.

We threw ourselves flat as the earth erupted in heat and flames and I felt a blow on my right hand. The raid continued, it seemed for an eternity, and then the drone of the aircraft receded...My first reaction was one of thankfulness that I had again survived. I then remembered the blow on my hand and held it up against the light of the moon. I saw that my little finger had gone and the one next to it was hanging by the flesh. ... I made my way to the hut we used as a hospital, stumbling as I went. I discovered to my surprise that my cotton trousers were wet with blood. I had also been hit in the thigh, taking away a piece of bone.

Bodies were lying around and I was placed by friendly hands on some kind of stretcher, a pad of cotton wool put over my hand and a bandage round my thigh. All this was done by the light of the moon and some coconut oil lamps. My friend Sergeant S. found me and reassured me as there was screaming where the doctors were doing emergency operations. My fear was that there would not be sufficient anaesthetic for all. Eventually my turn came. Cotton wool was placed over my mouth and something poured onto it. I was told to count ... my brain suddenly seemed to hit the sky.

I woke up in the hospital hut, feeling comfortably tired. I could leave it to the others now. ... Suddenly I remembered my hand and carefully felt where my fingers should be. Two had gone! Then my leg. That was bandaged. Friends came to see me and I learned that about one hundred men, British, Javanese and Dutch, had been killed around me and another three hundred injured. ...

The next morning we were loaded into lorries and friends saw us off. As we went, one told me he had found my little finger in his water can and that it had "a lovely fingernail!"... My other finger, I was told later, had been taken off with a pair of shears.

We eventually arrived at Nakon Pathon, a native village with a very big Buddhist temple. It was also a prison camp for very ill men. ... Very few men were fit enough to work and the food was very poor. We were a mixture of British, Australian, Dutch and Javanese.

I was placed in the hospital hut for treatment and my leg seemed to be healing, but my hand had become septic and swelled like a balloon. Colonel

We were in Manila for three weeks. A few had died and been buried at sea. Fifty of the original 750 were taken off as too sick. During a typhoon in the China Sea we got shipwrecked. Water broke through the steel side so we listed 30 degrees. Pumps in the engine room packed up and we had to bail out with 40-gallon drums. The Japs put ropes around their own waists, ready to jump overboard onto life rafts. There was a field gun in the stern, which they slewed round to point into the hold where we were, in case we were any trouble.

After a time, one engine was made to go and we managed to shift the boat onto an island. We had to stay aboard without food, as all the cookers and stores on the upper deck had been washed overboard. I had managed to acquire a bag of sugar somehow and we managed to exist on this for a bit. *[Sugar is supposed to prevent jaundice].*

Two big ice-boxes had smashed into each other in the storm and had burst open. They were found to contain pork, looking blue and green and some whitebait in similar condition. The pork was cut up and put into a stew for us. After four days we saw a Japanese warship on the horizon. It came towards us but couldn't quite get near enough to take us off, so an arrangement of lifeboat sails and ropes was made and ten men at a time were hauled to the big ship. As each man's turn came, he was tapped on the head with an oar to prevent trouble. When we reached the warship many of the men, me included, were too weak to climb the steep ladder to get aboard. Two Japs took you by the arms and threw you over the side onto the deck, like landing fish, and there you were shovelled aside with a pick axe handle to make room for the next.

Before leaving the shipwreck island we were each given one spoonful of cooked rice, the only food we had had for four days. Tea was made with salt water. On the warship there were big aluminium containers – bushel sized – of best white rice with whole fish. After so much starvation, we could only manage a mouthful or two of this. On Formosa we were offered the same again but still couldn't eat it. Many of them had dysentery and were just lying in their own muck on the deck. There they were off-loaded onto wooden lighters. As we jumped into them, fountains of water came up through shrapnel holes in the bottom. The lighters transferred us onto a lovely Japanese passenger ship, the *Haka-Sake Maru*. We hurried to the luxurious cabins only to be herded at the point of a bayonet into the straw-filled holds.

There were American submarine attacks every night and then the PoWs were rushed up on deck to be seen by US periscopes and perhaps prevent further attack. At that time we were surrounded by steel bulkheads, so you couldn't tell whether huge explosions were from rear-mounted 4 or 6-inch guns or from another submarine torpedo.

123

After a week, we reached Kobe in Honshu and from there went to Osaka by ferryboat to work in a shipbuilding yard. On March 18-19th 1945 Osaka was bombed from 11 pm until 6 am. Most of the town was destroyed by hundreds of 10 lb bombs with twelve sides. As they hit a surface they ignited and set off a propeller which sprayed petroleum liquid everywhere. Two huts, including mine were affected; everywhere around was burnt out. The burning pile of rubber tyres about 300 yards away was being used to cremate civilians from the town. From the light of this we could read the markings on low-flying US planes on March 19th 1945. One bomb took my hair off, but that was my only injury. Another came through a roof housing an American prisoner and went right through his chest and killed him.

In Osaka we experienced an earthquake. The Japs rushed to the nearest railway to sit on a sleeper. If the earth opened up under them the rail would straddle the gap. A brick pile near them shook and the bricks shattered. Piles of concrete bricks fell but didn't break and could be used again. Three horses, used to haul metal about, got killed. We had meat in our rations for days.

After being bombed out we went to Aome. ... Some prisoners had already been there for three years having gone straight from Singapore. They were making carbide in a blast furnace. It was used to drive civilian cars, as petrol and diesel were only for military use. Slag, coke and compressed coal "buns" were melted and poured into trucks then taken to be smashed into drums.'

Busty Rudd. 'We were loaded into the hold of the *Osaka Maru*. On the journey to Japan a typhoon hit us. We sprang a leak and a big fridge on the deck slithered into the sea and the ship foundered. We ran aground near Formosa and the hatch over the hold was opened – partly by the storm and partly by the Japs so we were able to get out.

I was picked up by a Japanese Corvette by breeches buoy. Some went onto other ships. We had to hang onto ropes all round the corvette until we could clamber aboard. We were taken to Osaka, where we were put to work on the docks. Our guard was an old gentleman. He was OK. I didn't mind him. He would hide us behind a factory and light a fire for us to sit beside.

Four prisoners were pushing a truck of rubbish along the dockside when the old boy shouted 'Stop! Stop!' It was an earthquake. We saw a factory chimney come down and all the Japs running out and onto the ships in the dock. The old man told us, 'When the earth open we go in and it close again over us.' The tremors lasted all night and only eased off the next morning. We did no work but just stood about till the shaking stopped, then it was off behind the factory again.

Our next work was in a carbide factor at Aome. There were big cylinders, which were loaded with lime and pitch and melted. The heat was so great that

124

the cylinders soon disintegrated and another had to be put over. This was done by prisoners who were suspended by straps and hooks and sat on a platform like a child's swing. From there, with boiling pitch below, they had to bolt on flanges to repair the cylinders. You had to stay suspended in this hot spot. Once I was so hot and sweaty I couldn't see and came out before the job was done. The Jap guard asked if the bolt was in place and when I said it was not I got such a belting. I was hit on the side of my face and knocked down onto the furnace platform then kicked, then sent back to work.'

Nelson Brighty. *From a letter written to his wife, Gladys, when he finally returned to England in February 1945.* 'I left Thailand in June 1944 for Singapore and there got a boat for Japan. We were crowded like rats, 650 in one hold. The heat was terrible. After 5 days travelling we reached Borneo and then the engine broke down. Eventually we made for Manila and reached there nine days later on 23rd July and there we were to stay till 20th September.

The first man died after 2 days of reaching there and when we left 92 had gone. Next day we were sunk by American planes and after being in the water for 6 hours I was picked up by a small fishing boat (the Japanese destroyers making off after they had picked up their own men) and was taken back to Manila to Bilbidid prison and that's how I came to be here at the right time. The villagers were all OK. It is going to be a happy day when I see you and Brian *[his son]* once more.'

Jim Quadling's mess tin, engraved with only a nail and a stone as a hammer.
This design was taken as the basis for the new memorial in Dereham market place, erected August 14 2005.

The Japanese

All Prisoner-of-War accounts contain many examples of Japanese (and Korean) brutality. Beatings were routine and beheadings common.

Charlie Frost. 'In a way, you couldn't blame them. The Japs had a national characteristic of cruelty. Their own troops got a hell of a beating if they did anything wrong. It was their rule'.

Busty Rudd. 'I often saw Jap private soldiers standing and bowing to their superior officers while they were being bashed up. I also saw Japanese children lining up in fours to go to school from an assembly point. If any got out of line the eldest child, aged perhaps 6, would have a bamboo stick and bash his colleagues into line again.

Once, in the factory, a Japanese private came over to speak to the prisoners and ask them where they had come from. He was a student at Cambridge University and had been in Japan on holiday when he was stopped from returning and put onto factory work. A guard saw him and gave him a real bashing with a bamboo stick. He was bowing and told them later he had been beaten because he shouldn't have left his machine.'

But not all Japanese were the same.

Jack Whitehead. *Working in the mines in Osaka.* 'We were allocated one-to-one to a Japanese civilian miner and you were to work with him in isolation. My co-worker was a man of about 40. I never knew his name and we had no common language but over the fifteen months we worked together we managed to communicate and used to jabber away.

When I first reached his little work platform I saw a huge compression drill and thought I would never be able to lift it, let alone work with it. I didn't have to!

My Jap motioned me to sit down, then lifted the drill himself and went to work. I did nothing but sit and watch for the whole fifteen months. As I got to understand my Jap better, he made me understand that he didn't believe the war should be happening, and didn't think the POW's should be ill-treated. The Jap insisted that I should say nothing to anyone, holding his lips together in his fingers. We would both have been in deep trouble if the situation was discovered. I never lifted a finger all that time. We got on like a house on fire, but I worried what would happen if he was ever sick and I had to work with another man. At Christmas 1944 we received our first ever Red Cross parcel, in which there was a big bar of chocolate, which I gave to his children. The Japs were no better off for food than we were. They were in a bad way.

126

After the war was over and the Americans had brought in supplies (by road, because an airdrop was impossible in that terrain) they had a party for all the Jap villagers. I met my Jap co-worker's wife and four children. They tried to persuade me to stay in Japan, saying "Japan is a good country."'

Hiroshima and the End of the War

Increased bombing by American planes had already given hope that the fortunes of the war were changing, though there was little firm news from the outside world. The dropping of the atom bomb changed everything.

Reg Anthony. *Working in a mine near Hiroshima.* 'I was in Hiroshima when the bomb fell. I think my life was saved by the depth of the mine. As I was brought up from the dark mine, at first I couldn't see, but when my sight adjusted I saw many dead people and many more in a terrible state.'

Busty Rudd. *In Osaka.* 'One of the prisoners had made a wireless, which was hidden in a bamboo. He heard that the Atomic Bomb had been dropped. We saw a Jap in an office weeping and then their guards all disappeared.'

Dick Langley. *At Phet Buri.* 'Outside our camp a little Chinese man used to push notes through the fence to us. Mostly they said "War finished", but on the last occasion it mentioned "the Bomb". No one had heard of this of course and neither had the guards, so we had to carry on as usual. Then suddenly the Japanese guards' attitude changed; they tried to get friendly and no work was demanded.'

Jack Whitehead. 'Suddenly there was a night with no bombers – it was 10 August 1945 and the Japs told us "no work today".

This silence continued for about a week, then the men who collected the rations were told by some Japs that there had been a big explosion – the Hiroshima bomb. We realised something was going on, but didn't know what. All our guards had disappeared.

We were called on parade and seven Japanese officers arrived in big cars, with uniforms covered in medals, and some interpreters. Some of the officers were very tall, but they put some steps and a platform for a short officer to address us. He announced "Hostilities have ceased." But wouldn't say straight out that they had surrendered and we had won.

Then our officers read out what was in the document. They told us two atomic bombs had been dropped, one in Hiroshima and one in Nagasaki.

They also said that the Americans were now in charge and would look after us. They added that "On September 3rd you were all to be executed. They couldn't afford to keep you.'"

Charles Frost. *In Saigon.* 'A few weeks after that they said the war was over and we went to a big camp – that was the finish. The guards disappeared overnight.

British Paratroopers came to Saigon, lovely boys. They handed out cigarettes. Chinese people came next with crates of chickens, but nobody wanted to pluck them. They also handed out 100-dollar bills, not worth much but it paid for a day out in Saigon.'

Fred Hoskins. *In the hospital camp at Nakon Pathon.* 'The word went round that a special bomb had been dropped in Japan killing thousands, something to do with Heavy Water. But camp routine continued. The sick helped the sick....

A small black plane flying high up, scattered leaflets and I was able to secure one. They fluttered down like silver sparks in the blue sky. Unfortunately, they were printed in Japanese and nobody in camp could read them. Later, Captain Escritt in England translated one for me. It was from the Emperor of Japan telling Japanese soldiers that it was not now a disgrace to surrender to the Allies....

Word passed round the camp that everyone should assemble in front of the stage. Something was up! There we were told that the war was over. There was spontaneous cheering and a Union Jack was produced from a hollow bamboo and hung up. A Dutch flag appeared from somewhere and was likewise hung up. We stepped over the bamboo boundaries into no-go areas and raided the Japanese stores for clothes. The Japanese flag was pulled down and the Union Jack now flown in its place on the camp flagpole.

The Japanese Commander's ducks were slaughtered and for once we had meat in our evening meal. We no longer bowed or saluted Japanese soldiers who generally kept to their quarters...

We heard a droning of aircraft and several Dakotas flew low over the camp. We could see the men inside them as they flew along the centre of the camp and pushed out food supplies and blankets. The blankets came down in bales and on hitting the ground, bounced high in the air. The food supplies came down by parachute and quite a few crashed through the roofs of the huts or into the pond. There was plenty for everyone. The whole situation seemed unreal. For so long we had been mistreated and starved that we had screwed our emotions down as a personal defence against hardship. Was it really the end or just some dream?

Many Japanese soldiers were returning from the jungle and they were in a bad way. They were given shelter in a hut on the far side of the camp. They were offered medical help by our doctors, but they refused it....

The Korean guards were given a house in the kampong and told by the Japanese to make their own way home!

That night we sat in the dark saying farewell to friends. We had very mixed emotions. We had been through a lot together and we didn't like the idea of leaving them [those not fit enough to travel immediately] behind. Was this really the end of our struggle to survive. It was three and a half years since we went into captivity...

When the morning came, we left the camp escorted by a Japanese guard, but this time with a difference. There was no shouting at us. The guard walked with his head down. We reached the village railway station and boarded the goods train that was standing there. Memories flooded back of an earlier journey. We sat bunched together on the floor and talked of our experiences as the train moved off.'

Reg Bullard. *In Osaka.* 'Better news for us on the 27 August, as an American plane was searching for our camp and others. The food improved in quality and quantity. I then weighed 9 stone 3½ pounds.

Over the next few days there was a series of food drops by USA planes and for once we all had plenty of food all the time. On 5 September we left Osaka by train and travelled to Yokohama where we were met by USAS officials and given more food and cigarettes. There followed medical tests; those who were considered fit enough spent the night on the landing craft, whilst those who were unfit went on to the hospital ship.'

Reggie Griffin. *In Osaka.* 'On *[August]* 16th the Japs gave us soap, cigs and tobacco, toilet paper more than we have had before. ... I also received a card from home after so long without one. Today the Japs came round with an armful of bootlaces. ... Before they would give us about six pair for 38 men, but now the boot is on the right foot. ... We are still waiting for further orders to move, the sooner the better to get out of this country. We've had a bath every day since we've been free men.

On Thursday 23rd the army guards took over the camp. The Japs are putting a wooden platform on the roof of the building and painting P.W. on it. Heard that our planes were coming to drop food supplies on the 25th and about eight o'clock we saw 12 planes coming over. So we all rushed out on to the square and they encircled the camp and was it nice to see them again! ... A little more excitement this afternoon; two or three big planes flying around dropping food supplies, some of the boys have gone out to get it into camp. Soon as they brought it in we got a packet of Raleigh, clothes, boots, chocolate, chewing gum. The boys were smoking and singing all night.

On the 30th two more planes came over with some more food, dropped it right against the camp this time on the mountain side .... One Jap got killed; a box of chewing gum hit him on the head.'

Jack Whitehead. 'The Americans took over a big hall but there was no piano and we wanted to have a sing-song. Someone said there was one in the school so they purloined it, stopped the first lorry to come by and brought it back to No. 4 camp.

At 2 pm each day the Americans announced in turn each separate camp's future movement. No. 4 camp was not mentioned for about 4 weeks. At last they told us we were off tomorrow. Lorries took us to Osaka station bound for Tokyo. We stopped with a jerk at Hiroshima, an awful sight. We could see white-coated figures with red crosses on. I never want to see anything like that again.

Then we arrived at Tokyo docks and boarded a US destroyer for Manila. As we went on deck the Americans just grabbed our clothes and threw them overboard, "You don't want those any more." Then they kitted us out again. It was an emotional moment as we left Japan; so many men were not coming back with us.

They don't hang about, those Americans; we went through eight separate showers, with first water, then soap powder, then rinses. We had been ragamuffins before, now we were in clean white shirts and shorts.

We went to the radio room aboard to send cables home. No one could send any individual messages. You just gave your name and address and they sent "Safe in Allied hands. Home soon. Love Jack." Then there were days waiting for a reply. None of us knew anything about our families at home. A cable came at last, the same for each of us, "So pleased. See you soon."'

Special Characters

Dr Harold Churchill

Reg Anthony. 'He was the one who kept a diary on rice paper and buried it in a tin wherever he went'.

This in itself was an act of courage, for the keeping of records of any sort was forbidden by the Japanese.

Sidney Greenwood. *From an interview with Raymond Greenwood, his son.* 'My father was captured in Singapore. He was wounded with shrapnel in the left

THE WAR OFFICE,
CURZON STREET HOUSE,
CURZON STREET,
LONDON, W.I.

5. 9. 45.

MADAM,

I am directed to inform you with pleasure that official information has been received that your HUSBAND 5772840. PTE. J. O. QUADLING, THE ROYAL NORFOLK REGIMENT previously a prisoner of war in Japanese hands, has been recovered and is now with the Allied Forces.

The repatriation of recovered Prisoners of War is being given highest priority, but it will be appreciated that some time must elapse before they reach the United Kingdom. Information of a general character regarding these recovered prisoners, including their movements before they reach home, will be given from time to time on the wireless and will be published in the press.

I am, MADAM,

Your obedient Servant.

A J Weston

MRS J. O. QUADLING.
"WELL HOUSE"
NORWICH ROAD,
YAXHAM,
DEREHAM,
NORFOLK.

Letter from the War Office informing Mrs Quadling that her husband was safe in allied hands.

calf. Doctor Churchill operated on him in Singapore and managed to take out the shrapnel, but there was a lot of damage to the leg tissue. I remember a scar on the back of my father's leg stretching about 4" x 3" over the calf. It was covered with very thin skin like tissue paper and you could see veins and muscles through it. When he got home after the war, the leg caused a great deal of pain. I think from gangrene. He went to the Norfolk and Norwich Hospital where Mr Birt operated on him – at first, removing two toes. Then he had to have a below knee amputation and eventually the leg was taken off at mid thigh.

On one occasion later on he had further pain and sent for his Dereham doctor. Doctor Churchill appeared at the door and this began a friendship and they used to meet and reminisce. Neither man was one to make much of his memories. I occasionally overheard their conversation. I remember them talking about the Japs' very cruel treatment, such as bamboo spikes being pushed under fingernails. And they mentioned the railway. That's where they got beaten.' .

'Weary' Dunlop
['The War Diaries of Weary Dunlop' were published in 1986]

Harry Cassidy. *In Java.* 'The prisoner in charge of all the rest of them was 'Weary Dunlop' who was a very well respected Australian surgeon...

Then we were moved to Dola Rosa camp, where he *[Dunlop]* was treating many wounded men including Bill Griffiths who took a lot of nursing. He had been sent to an outlying island where he was blown up by a landmine and had lost both hands and both eyes. Weary Dunlop patched him up and he is now in St Dunstan's.'

From a reference in a letter to Fred Hoskins from Ewart Escritt, it appears that Fred was also operated on by Weary Dunlop. See page 114.

Colonel Lilley T.D. CO 1/5th Battalion Sherwood Foresters

Jack Whitehead. 'Col. Lilley was small in stature, but a giant in every other respect. The interest of the men was always his first thought. He achieved a lot by saying very little. There were several times during our PoW days that he clashed with the Japanese, over something they had done to one of us, or about something he did not agree with, and he often had his way. The regiment was split up during the railway work, and we all lost track of each other. I know that Col. Lilley survived the war, but that he died not long after we came home. A fine man was lost when he went.'

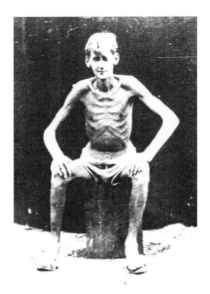

A prisoner in an advanced stage of malnutririon

Homecoming

Organising transport for all the prisoners took time. Those who were fit to travel went first, others being hospitalised for a while until their condition improved. Many had lost up to six stone in weight. All were suffering from malnutrition and much more besides. They travelled by air and sea to the west coast of the North America, then by train across the continent. Many arrived at Liverpool or Southampton in October 1945, but some were not home until December.

Charlie Frost. 'We refuelled in Bangkok and went on to Rangoon where we were put in hospital. There were nurses and chocolates and things, but we wanted to look round Rangoon. Mountbatten came to welcome us.

After a week we boarded a French ship crewed by Yorkshire boys. I helped in the galley and they really looked after me. When we arrived in Liverpool, we were given kit bags loaded up with sugar and fruit and chocolate – all the things you couldn't get in England, to take home. We were met by friendly policemen who grabbed the packs off our backs and carried them.

Next stop was a camp in Northampton for a few weeks' recuperation and assessment. I finally got home in October 1945.'

Reggie Griffin. 'Now at last we have arrived at Victoria, Canada. What a welcome! Before we got anywhere near the docks the air raid sirens were blowing on every ship. People all over the docks and two bands, navy band and army band.'

Jack Whitehead. 'In Manila we stayed in marquees, 50 of us in each. Japs were working there as servants and cleaners. We were all urged to say, "it's all over now."

My normal weight is around 10 stone. As I got on the boat in Manila I weighed 6 stone, as I left it I was 11 stone. Doctors in Manila examined all the prisoners. If they were very ill they were sent to Australia to recuperate and arrangements were made for their wives to join them.

Those who were thought fit enough to go straight home, me among them, were taken to HMS *Implacable*, an aircraft carrier, under Captain Fox. He spoke to us as soon we had all boarded and told us, "From now on you are all passengers, rather than prisoners – you are not wanted to do any work at all." We had wonderful care.

We refuelled at Honolulu and saw Pearl Harbor. We were not allowed ashore but girls came out to us and put leis round our necks.'

[After crossing the Rockies by plane] 'We ended back in Halifax, Nova Scotia and were told we could have anything we liked from the NAAFI. Then with only two days to go before we sailed the Canadian government gave us 80 dollars, which had to be spent in Canada. I bought myself a watch, but still had a lot of the money. Then someone suggested filling a kit bag with all the things you couldn't get in England, so I filled up with chocolate, soap, tobacco, etc. ... On 22 October 1945 we boarded a French ship, the *Ile de France* their crack ship. The ship was lovely, but the French didn't put themselves out to make us welcome. ....

I reached home on 1st November 1945. I was met at Waterloo Station by my wife and my father and her father. Me and my wife were put into a taxi, but the two older men had to make their own way back.

As we got to our house, all I wanted was a cup of tea and some peace with my wife. But there was a welcoming party of about 30 relatives and friends. Some 4 ½ hours later they had all left and we just sat and talked for the rest of the night.'

Busty Rudd. 'We finally got home by boat to Tokyo, US plane to Okinawa and onto Nova Scotia and Jamaica. The Lady Nelson brought us to Southampton. There we stayed in camp for about three weeks having examinations and tests and finally were given railway passes. Train to Norwich. Car home, finally arrived at midnight. My weight on enlistment was between 11 and 12 stone. I went down to 5 stone and was only 6 stone when I got home.'

Reg Bullard. 'We were flown to Okinawa and then left Manila on the troopship *Admiral Hugh Rodman* on the 18 September and sailed to San Francisco and were welcomed by a display of fireboats and bands playing. We spent two days sightseeing, getting fixed up with British uniform. We travelled across America by train on the Santa Fe Railway to New York where we did more sightseeing. We sailed for home on the *Queen Elizabeth* and whilst en route the USA sent telegrams home and received answers whilst on board ship.

We arrived at Southampton at 9.30am on 18 October 1945. There was no welcome bands etc. only transport to the transit camps. We stayed overnight and then continued the homeward journey and I finally reached home at 9.45pm on 19 October 1945, at last!'

Bertie Boyce. 'Basil Leggett, who lived up in Cemetery Road was killed in a dreadful accident. He was still up in Thailand. The war was just over and a few American bombers flew over dropping supplies. One container hit the hut he was in and he was one of several killed. This was just three days after we were told it was all over. Men who were POWs were on the way home in a bomber plane when a terrible accident happened. Somehow the bomb doors opened and these poor chaps fell into the Pacific Ocean.

Mother had my bed ready when she heard we were coming home. She found me fast asleep on the floor, thinking I had fallen out of bed. I told her that I couldn't sleep in a bed, never having had a proper bed for about 4 years.'

Fred Hoskins. 'Our first stop was when we docked at Colombo in Ceylon. Then to a stretch of desert alongside the shore of the Red Sea where there was a Forces Depot at an incredible place called Adabiya. Here everything was laid on for those returning from the Far East: clothing, entertainment etc. ...We were kitted out with two of everything to the extent that I struggled with two loaded kitbags plus other odds and ends...

At some time we were issued with notices not to speak to the press and given forms to complete regarding details of escapes, or attempted escapes, P/W deaths and other casualties, British or American personnel who helped the enemy and War Crimes. I still have these forms....

With the minimum of delay we sailed through the Bay of Biscay and up to Liverpool where we ran into fog and had to anchor outside the harbour for the night. In the morning, we docked and were amazed to see crowds lining the dockside. Those of us lining the handrail tried to identify loved ones and a microphone was being passed round on the dock for people to shout messages. I remember one in particular where the message was, "You wait till you come home!" It sounded almost like a threat for having been away so long. Again the feeling of uncertainty. Time had moved on and we had to get up to date. Things had changed during our absence.

Then we landed and were taken to the railway station from where we went our different ways. Strangely at this time we felt little real emotion. We finally arrived at Norwich railway station where again we found there was a crowd waiting for us. A woman in a fur coat threw her arms around me and kissed me! Men seized my kitbags and I was taken to a waiting car. "Where to?" I was asked.

It was quite dark when we arrived at the cottage in Elsing. I invited my befrienders into the cottage but they refused and disappeared into the darkness. I went in the cottage and was re-united with my wife and saw my baby son for the first time. I then realised that I was really home. The nightmare had ended.

I had been away four years and four days.'

After the War

All the returned prisoners, to a greater or lesser degree, suffered the effects of their years of deprivation, physical, emotional and psychological. This obviously affected their families as well.

Jack Whitehead. 'My son John had only been nine months old when I went away; now he was nearly five years old. Although he had been shown photographs of his father, and told about him, he still asked his mother "Who is that man and how long is he staying?"

It took eight or nine months for Jack to begin to get over his wartime experiences. Very sadly, son John died of sepsis following an appendix operation at the age of 18. A daughter was born in 1957 and Jack and his wife have come to live in Dereham to be near her.

Many were reluctant to talk about their experiences. Sue Palmer records that when she interviewed **Busty Rudd**, *'All through Busty's story his wife had been quietly listening to it. She had never heard it before.'*

Dick Langley. *General comment on survivors.* 'The skinny ones did best. They had been brought up on food served little and good'.

Nightmares were a common occurrence.

Bertie Perkins. *From Bertie's widow, Gladys.* 'Bertie and I were engaged before the war, but had to wait till he returned from the Far East to get married. Bertie had nightmares when he got home. Once I woke to find his hands round my throat. I dared not move because I really thought he might hurt me in his dream. I just kept calling out "Bertie, Bertie,". When he woke up he said, "I thought I'd got my hands round a Jap's neck. If you had struggled, I'd have strangled you."

Another time I found him trying to climb out of the window to escape the Jap guards in a nightmare.'

Dick Osborne. 'When I finally got home I went back to working as a slaughterer for the Ministry of Food but I found I was not strong enough to carry on. In 1948 I went to 'Hobbies' as an engineer bench worker.

My wife now, though not at the time, was Edna Bales, who was also at Hobbies doing war work as a capstan operator. Edna used to go to and from work on her bike, which had a funny sized tyre – 26" x 1 ". She needed a new one and was told "Ask Dick, he'll get you one." I did, the same night. We were married in 1950.'

Edna's brother, Sidney, had also been a prisoner of war. He died, aged 23, on August 16th 1943.

Joe Mason. *From an interview with Fred Mason, Joe's son.* 'One Jap guard in charge of Changi camp was a right arse-hole and would beat up anyone, any time. He was a particularly nasty Jap. He went alone into the jungle one day and Joe knifed him, then buried his body. There was no enquiry, as it was assumed that he had absconded.

Joe was widowed a few years after his return. His wife died in childbirth. He lived alone thereafter, but sometimes turned up in the night at my house or my sister's, having had a nightmare and been unable to settle after that. Eventually his mind began to go and he spent the last few years of his life in St Andrew's Hospital, Thorpe, Norwich. My wife and I went to fetch him every weekend and he would spend Saturday and Sunday at our home.

One weekend, the doctor there asked to speak to me. He wanted to know what my father had told me about the war. The answer was "Nothing." The doctor then revealed that all his father's mental disturbances had been due to his memories and guilt about killing the Jap guard. He sometimes went into a sort of trance from which no one could rouse him. When he was like that we could not take him home.'

137

Sue Palmer. *Joe died on 21st March 1985 and his death certificate shows the causes of death as: Chronic anaemia, Hiatus hernia, Chronic anxiety state. It does not say that the first was probably caused by continued infestation with intestinal worms, or that any of the causes resulted from his FEPOW experiences.*

Forgive and Forget?

George Parnell. *From his widow, Mrs Beryl Parnell, always known as Grace.* 'George wouldn't have anything Japanese in the house.'

Fred Hoskins. 'Sometimes I am asked, "Isn't it time you forgot all this? After all, it happened a long time ago." The simple answer is "No". A traumatic experience, such as you have read about, changes the whole course of one's life. We were constantly told we would never go home again and see our loved ones. We were beaten, starved and used brutally as slave labour. Our clothes rotted and were not replaced. The light of hope was extinguished for some, but for the rest of us, the tiny flame was nourished in the human warmth of friendship and unity among our fellow prisoners who shared our miserable existence.

To forgive is a different matter. When I came home, I was bitter and hated all things Japanese. I refused to see a group of Japanese who visited the school to see our educational methods.

Over the years I have had time to reflect. I have no hate of the younger generation of Japanese who were not involved, but it would be a betrayal of my comrades, who died in ruthless Japanese hands so far from home, if I truly said "I forgive them". I just feel neutral. I do not want revenge. I do feel a great sadness at the totally unnecessary loss of young men who were the flower of our country and the unnecessary suffering that was caused.'

Bill Garrod. 'Padre Duckworth eventually became a Canon at Cambridge University. He was known as The Red Canon. Jim Quadling and I went to a reunion in Coggeshall after the war. In the speeches we heard a War Office wallah saying we should "forgive and forget." Duckworth gave him a rollicking. Then another officer said, "If I was the Bishop I would have fired the Canon long ago."'